'In today's day and age, with social media being everywhere and around you all the time, sometimes it's easier for influencers to get a bad reputation, but if there's an argument against that, I think it's Masoom Minawala's work. I think she is consistent, hard-working, and I really admire how she sticks by her guns to who she is and has created her own niche. I think she is a very intelligent businesswoman, and I really admire her work ethic.' – **Rhea Kapoor**

'You have the right to work, but never to the fruit of the work.'

– Lord Krishna, Bhagavad Gita

SHE'LL NEVER MAKE IT

SHE'LL NEVER MAKE IT

My Journey from Doubt to Dominance

Masoom Minawala

with

Aditi Shah Bhimjyani

🌸 juggernaut

JUGGERNAUT BOOKS
C-I-128, First Floor, Sangam Vihar, Near Holi Chowk,
New Delhi 110080, India

First published by Juggernaut Books 2024

10 9 8 7 6 5 4 3 2 1

P-ISBN: 9789353458522
E-ISBN: 9789353458133

Typeset in Brandon Grotesque by R. Ajith Kumar, Noida

Printed at Replika Press Pvt. Ltd, India

To my Mom and Dad

CONTENTS

INTRODUCTION

'She'll never make it . . .'

This is something I've heard a lot throughout my life.

I still believe I have a long way to go before I do make it, but somewhere along the way, in the attempt to prove everyone wrong, I found that when you wear your heart on your sleeve, your passion on your fingertips and your conviction on your lips, things turn out okay.

To introduce myself – I am a content creator, influencer, entrepreneur and investor, with 1.4 million followers and two businesses.

My USP is the impact or conversion – when a viewer or reader takes an action that brings value to a business (like clicking on a link or making a purchase) – I drive today despite the sense of mediocrity that has dogged me most of my life.

Throughout my life I've craved to belong. I've had multiple shortcomings and countless failures. I've constantly been reminded of everything I was not and could not be. Little moments of weakness that built into gaping holes of insecurity.

This book is about the sheer magic of stumbling upon the career of your dreams and having the balls to chase that dream over and over and over again until you make it come true.

This book is the story of a girl who found herself through her work. And most importantly, the story of a girl who ultimately realized that it didn't matter if they thought she would make it or not.

This is my story, and nobody gets to write it for me.

This is my story, and I promise to tell it with radical honesty.

ONE

THE INTERNSHIP THAT CHANGED MY LIFE

I was an Average Jane, and this is my story.

Creating content has been and will always be my first and true love. It began with fashion, and while staying centred around it even now, it has branched into my life, my businesses, my beauty diary, my family, my experiences, my travel and so much more.

That I managed to turn it into a super successful (and lucrative) business model is the icing on the cake.

But how did all this start?

Well, I started my fashion blog Style Fiesta on a whim, overnight, as an 18-year-old college kid. I held on to it with my entire being, through the ups and downs of life, over more than a decade. And I believe it's taken me this far. I don't just mean that it is an accomplishment by the book, but it has given me a sense of pure fulfilment. When I stumbled upon a 'blog' for the very first time in my life, you know what attracted me to it the most? It was the fact that anyone from anywhere around the world could watch, share and comment on something I was creating sitting in a corner of India. I just couldn't fathom that kind of connectedness. That sense of community. A sense of belonging.

It felt like coming home.

THE BEGINNING

I grew up in a pretty hardcore Gujarati business family, a joint one at that, in midtown Mumbai, Prabhadevi to be precise. I have one sibling, an older brother. We shared our home with my paternal grandparents and, for the first 13 years of my life, also with my father's two siblings and their two children. My early days were spent with nine other people in a cramped house with warm memories of watching *Mahabharata* on Sundays and my mother feeding me with her right hand and my brother with her left. It was a brimming, happy household.

My brother and I grew up on mattresses on the floor of my parents' room. I would secretly watch some late-night TV, so I was grateful for this arrangement! Plus, I got to crawl into my parents' bed for the cosiest of mornings. In fact this is an exercise that I haven't let go of even as a 30-year-old woman. If you were to walk into my Mumbai

My early teens

From the archives

home on a Sunday afternoon you would find me napping, cosied up between my parents. My husband always makes fun of this habit but I secretly think he's just jealous. We grew up financially comfortable, or at least I was always made to think so. I knew not to have too many demands, yet I had more than enough to be grateful for.

My father was a man of determination (he still is) and his journey began with almost nothing. But he made it. This became a strong foundation for me growing up. **If you work hard and keep working hard, you most probably will make it. I had proof right in front of my eyes.**

My grandfather had opted for an early retirement, and the entire responsibility of our family was on my father who dreamt of starting a diamond jewellery business. My mother, meanwhile, ran her own silver jewellery business. My parents would pull all-nighters in the factory my dad had painstakingly set up with borrowed capital. They travelled to different cities trying to find clients, leaving us in the comforting arms of Dadima and Dadu. They worked so hard and we could see it. That was in fact my very first, most vivid memory of ambition and hard work.

Of course, hard work translating into success isn't guaranteed for everyone and I've learned that with time. A few years in the business would go on to teach me that

I also had the social, educational and cultural privilege of being able to spot a market opportunity and 'work hard' to translate it into success. And I am aware of and grateful for all the wonderful things this privilege has brought into my life.

My parents are the type who have always encouraged my brother and me to follow our hearts. There was no pressure to 'do' anything, personally, professionally, romantically – we were allowed to be. I guess that too has its strengths and weaknesses. I was confident but underachieving. I was reasonably street smart but never excelled.

My summers were spent in Nagpur with my maternal grandparents. I loved the small-town life and I was spoilt rotten with love and affection and buckets of Haldiram's rasgullas by my nani, mama, mami and cousins. We always cried when we had to leave. I remember thinking to myself, I would love to live in a town like this, where you knew the person in the car at a traffic light, where there was one eating hotspot and the whole neighbourhood would dine there on a Saturday night. Funny thing is, years later, when I walked into my husband's home in Belgium for the first time after being engaged to him, I found myself staring at the exact same spiral staircase as the one in my nani's house and a hauntingly similar 'small town' life. It's crazy how we subconsciously manifest what we wish for, even if it's decades later.

When I was a pre-teen and teenager, my mom would often take me shopping to Dadar (a busy residential suburb in central Mumbai) market – part resembling Delhi's Janpath and part Chandni Chowk. I once suggested to her that maybe we should upgrade to the Hill Road market (an avenue of semi-street and semi-stall shopping spots in the chic western suburb of Bandra) because a friend bought cute jeans from there, and that became our newly discovered mom–daughter shopping spree spot. I would buy the coolest hipster jeans for ₹200 and it felt like all my fashion dreams had been fulfilled. We'd sneak in a round at Clothes Rack too, a factory-reject discount store for all the popular high-street things I aspired to own.

If you had asked that girl then whether she could envision herself dressed by Hermes, Valentino or the best designer names in India, Dubai or Paris – the answer would have probably been a resounding no. It was not something I imagined. It wasn't a childhood fantasy that turned into reality. As you read along, you'll notice it was more of a wing-it-at-every-curveball dream that I never even dared to dream.

My brother and I went to Bombay Scottish School. I was an average student with ordinary grades. If someone asked me what my favourite subject was, I would promptly say 'None!' I was more dedicated to football than academics. I loved the adrenaline of being on the ground, defending a goal like my life depended on it (I played centre defence) and some might even say I was mildly aggressive on the field. I remember desperately wanting to make captain and marching up to my coach and asking him when he was going to make me one. 'I've been performing on the field,' I said. He said, 'You don't become captain by performing in matches. You become captain by showing up for every single practice and showing your team you are committed.' This was probably my first lesson in understanding that showing up and consistency, especially on the unimportant days, could go a long way. I finally made captain in the last term of grade 10 and I THRIVED. Being a leader excited every bone in my body. My first experience with the power of self-talk was also on the field. I would walk on to the ground and repeat in my mind 'We're going to win today' over 50 times. Obviously, we didn't win every match, but a loss never stopped me from repeating the exercise the next match day either. I was sporty but also creative. I loved dancing, painting, sketching, drawing and – at the risk of confirming my dorkiness – making scrapbooks. I did feel like I had some inclination towards fashion and, at some point, fashion design was on my mind. But it was an undeveloped little inkling.

My other big inclination was towards technology. There was one computer in my house, and it stayed in my grandfather's room. He was extremely tech-savvy and technically it was his computer, but we always fought over who would get to use it more. Sometimes he would say embarrassing things to me in front of my friends or get upset if I hadn't spent enough time with him. The making up, though, was my favourite part. He was supremely adaptive and he stayed that way until he passed away in 2021. Glued to his computer screen and always adapting with technology. I guess I got this from him.

YOUNG, DUMB AND LISTLESS

Soon enough, post grade 10, I found myself at HR College in Mumbai. Unfortunately, I barely ever made it to class. I was bored, aimless and at the brink of my crucial grade 12 board exams when I also had to decide what I wanted to do next. A deep sense of dissatisfaction and helplessness had set in. Skipping class and spending your college life in the canteen eating Chinese fried rice feels like a dream until you realize two years have gone by, all your friends are off to universities abroad or studying for their CA exams, and your only future plan is going to Colaba Causeway for some street shopping the following Monday.

This was also the time in my life when my confidence was at its absolute lowest. I had a falling out with my friends from school which was a scene right out of a teen TV drama and, in all honesty, it mentally shattered me. My mom was worried about me and I would overhear her on the phone expressing how she didn't know what to do to pull me out of this low. I don't quite remember how I dealt with it because the mind has a way of deleting some memories, but I do remember it scarring me, robbing me of any self-esteem I had and making me feel very, very alone. What did I take away from that incident? That surely there was something wrong with me.

Sadly, there's nobody to tell you that you will get past this and the best friends you could ever imagine await you on the other side. That's the thing with bad stuff, right? The only way to escape it is to actually just live it.

Now, just team up that loneliness with a lack of

purpose and you don't have a winning combination. I really needed to 'do something' with my life. I did not think I had what it takes to pursue a typical professional field. I truly did not believe I had the bandwidth to cope up with the education that was required to become a doctor, engineer, lawyer, architect, etc. It might have something to do with my maths teacher in school who, in the presence of 15 other classmates, had boldly announced that I should become a dancing girl, because I was surely not good for anything else. Of course, I was upset. And before I knew it, her words had suddenly turned into a belief for me. That I was good for nothing.

I did the rounds at some local colleges to see if I could figure something out with fashion marketing or merchandising but there were no options back then. I had no idea what I was going to do next. Was I about to spend the next few years achieving zilch? I was already waking up in the early afternoons and whiling away my time. I went back to HR College to sign up for a three-year BCom degree. I distinctly remember the feeling while filling in the admission form – I was so disappointed. The course did not excite me at all and I knew I was meant for more than this. Why couldn't I find a path I could flourish in?

I decided to pick up other courses on the side. That was the silver lining I found in a BCom degree – the luxury of time to pursue other interests. I borrowed my friend's camera and took up a one-week photography course. I thought to myself – this is fun – how about doing another course? I signed up for a diploma in fine arts at Rachna College in Mumbai. I could handle the timings along with my BCom degree. I was so excited. I figured this would appeal to my creative soul and bring my education together with something I was passionate about. But, as it turned out, I hated it. I didn't have the courage to tell my parents that I couldn't see the course through. I lied to my family for the rest of the year saying I was going to Rachna College, but instead I spent hours at a friend's house . . . doing just about nothing.

Somewhere around this time, the insecurity I was feeling started solidifying. I was constantly comparing myself to others and to others' lives and I simply did not feel good enough.

Anyway, the mediocrity continued, until there came a day that I didn't want the same life. I woke up and I just knew I had to change something. And there's a very important lesson I learnt here. This was a moment of immense, game-changing strength. The willingness to change. **That one moment of strength can outweigh a dozen moments of weakness**. For me, that moment of strength came in the form of feeling absolutely useless in HR College and wanting to do something about it. **Hold on to those moments because in a life filled with the background hum of corrosive and constant self-doubt and insecurity, these moments of actually wanting to upend the game and change are hard to come by. And when they do, and you find the power to act on them, that's life altering.**

THE DAY I FOUND LOVE

I decided in that moment to apply for internships. Maybe studying wasn't for me but surely some on-ground work experience could be? I scrambled for an internship (I was 19 and still in college) and after a dozen applications, I finally landed one. I got an interview at one of India's leading retail groups.

The office was lavish and sprawling and everyone showed up in suits and crisp shirts and you had to mark your attendance with a digital ID. It was out of my league and I felt honoured to have some role to play in this fancy-shmancy world. It was also my very first paid opportunity;

₹5,000 was my stipend for a month in 2011–12. I felt like I had landed gold.

The hours felt long, my body felt exhausted and yet I loved how hectic it was – I was finally mentally and physically being put to good use. I learnt branding, marketing, visual merchandising: *the business side of fashion.* And I abso-freakin-lutely loved it. The discovery was quick. I had a sense of purpose.

My boss at the time was someone we were all petrified of. Funny thing – a few years after my internship, while I was full swing into the content-creation game – she happened to switch careers and start a blog herself. I remember her reaching out to me with questions and for guidance and it truly felt like things had come full circle. But that was far in the future still – let's go slow.

A month into work, my boss called a meeting and told our team that one of the global brands we managed had briefed her on 'bloggers' and how it was becoming a rapidly growing marketing avenue for the brand. We needed to do a research project on how we could apply the same strategy to the Indian market. She assigned this project to me. I nodded my head even though I had no idea what blogging even meant. I was too scared to express my ignorance. The only time I had heard of a 'blog' was through Amitabh Bachchan and something about his father's poems, and I was pretty sure my boss wasn't referring to that.

I scampered back to my desk with my head down and googled the five words that would go on to change my life. 'What is a fashion blog?'

What I saw in front of me (sorry to be dramatic) took my breath away. This was love at first sight kind of love. The 'LET'S DROP EVERYTHING AND START A FASHION BLOG' kind of love.

I was captivated. I didn't look up from my screen for five hours. Fashion blogging was a different world back then. There were beautiful, interactive websites with six to seven vivid, stylish images of one outfit. It was followed by a few paragraphs of text filled with fashion opinions, perspectives and trend reports, the blogger's personality simply oozing out of each word and carefully curated photograph. With filters and graphics, you could select and see things thematically. On the side were lovely widgets, banners and stickers to follow the blogger on Myspace or different platforms. It was basically a visual magazine of an individual's content. I was enamoured and wanted to step into these pages. I discovered only one fashion blogger from India, though. Her name was

Arushi Khosla and she took her photos on the terrace of her Delhi home. While scrolling through her work, my mind connected the dots. I realized fashion blogging was also possible this close to home.

That evening, my mind was racing all through the 45-minute taxi ride home. I told my parents I had to do this stuff as it was 'just next level and so cool'. I wanted to start my own fashion blog.

My parents didn't quite understand it, but they're the kind of people who don't ask too many questions. They just went with it. (You'll notice this pattern when it comes to my family in my journey. A pattern of just going with it. Allowing me to make my own mistakes and being onlookers. And in a world of overly opinionated conversations, constant overanalysing or 'log kya kahenge' [what will people say], I sincerely hope this pattern of theirs is one I can pass on to my children.)

My mom came up with my blog name in 20 minutes. Style Fiesta. **And that very night, glued to the item that would go on to become my best friend – my laptop – I started my own fashion blog.**

I didn't sleep a wink that night. There was a platform called blogger.com to create your own blog. This is the stuff you'd hire people to do for you today but at that time I was enthusiastic and, as you already know, tech-inclined. I spent the night learning PHP, which is a widely used open source scripting language for websites, so I could format and create my own blog. It's safe to say I went bleary-eyed to work for the next many mornings. But at least I now knew how to code!

This 'blog' that was simply a passionate hobby back then helped me find myself. And maybe that's the reason this business I have built today, which has its roots in my blog, is so close to my heart.

I played around with so many ideas over the years, and most didn't stick. I was a bit of a serial entrepreneur and you'll soon read how and why! But I kept at it. **From my perspective, the only way you can redefine your story is by taking that first step**. I could have easily just stayed in awe of the first fashion blog I saw from a safe distance. But **I noticed something I loved. I saw something that made me want to stay up all night to learn how to code! So I took the first step towards making it happen. And that action, that step, was how I began to live the life of my dreams.**

TAKE EVERY CHANCE THAT COMES YOUR WAY

It was ultimately that marketing internship that changed my life. But when I look back, it could have been any of the moments in my journey. You see – it's not always a eureka moment. It could just as well be a tiny choice you make on any given day. It could have been the fine arts course, it could have been something from my BCom degree, it could have been another internship I did with my mom's friend. But **if you don't get out of your comfort zone and live the bad stuff, you'll never know which of those can turn out to be the good stuff.**

In terms of practical advice for all the school and college students out there: **do as many internships as you can. In whatever field you are interested in.** Whether you're a statistician or a furniture maker. Whether you're a biomedical engineer or a journalist. Do whatever internship you can grab. **Cold email people. (Make sure to attach your CV and write an unexpected, quirky, memorable covering letter.) Use your friends and family networks.** Experience through internships is invaluable. You learn not only the nuts and bolts of how work actually happens and how organizations function, but also how to behave and act in those environments – small hidden codes and norms that you can't get unless you get out there. (For instance, a print journalist friend of mine told me if you dress too posh and polished in a newsroom, you'll stick out like a sore thumb. Who knew?!). Soak it all in. Internships are the tasting menu of life.

TWO

I FAILED AND HIT ROCK BOTTOM TOO

**Failure and defeat define the game
as much as the win.**

Let me take you back to the first two times I ever created content in my life. The first was sub-consciously and then, consciously. Both were with my late grandfather.

The first time, I was seven years old and doing a lavani dance performance in my neighbourhood. I got ready and my dadu came with his retro camera and we did a 20-minute photoshoot. I think that was the real start of my love affair with photographs.

The second time was the morning of 11 December 2011. The day before, I had stumbled upon the word 'fashion blog' for the first time, and I had stayed up that entire night setting up my blog and learning how to code. Because hello, world-before-Shopify-and-Wix, you needed to know how to code to set up your own website! Once I set up the internal systems, I marched up to Dadu and told him I wanted to start a fashion blog for which I needed a camera. I knew he would get it; I was his soft corner. It was technology-related and he rarely said no to me for anything. I knew how to use my charm with the old man. He took me into the smallest lanes of a busy suburban electronics market and bought me a camera and a tripod.

EVERYBODY STARTS SOMEWHERE

I would place the camera in my room in front of my cupboard, try on different outfits, take photos using the remote trigger and upload them on my blog. Thereafter, I'd spend hours writing the text. I would talk about what trend I was identifying, why I paired x with y. I borrowed my mother's pearls and dressed them up. I took my brother's shirt and wrote a trend report on borrowing from a man's closet. I was having a blast.

I soon yearned for better quality photos, so I started requesting other people to shoot for me – anyone who I felt was slightly inclined towards photography was my target, including the friends of my parents and neighbours from my building. I didn't overthink the photos I was putting up of myself. Back then, I wasn't very critical of myself or my body or how an image looked. I knew I wasn't a supermodel by any stretch of the imagination –

My StyleFiesta office

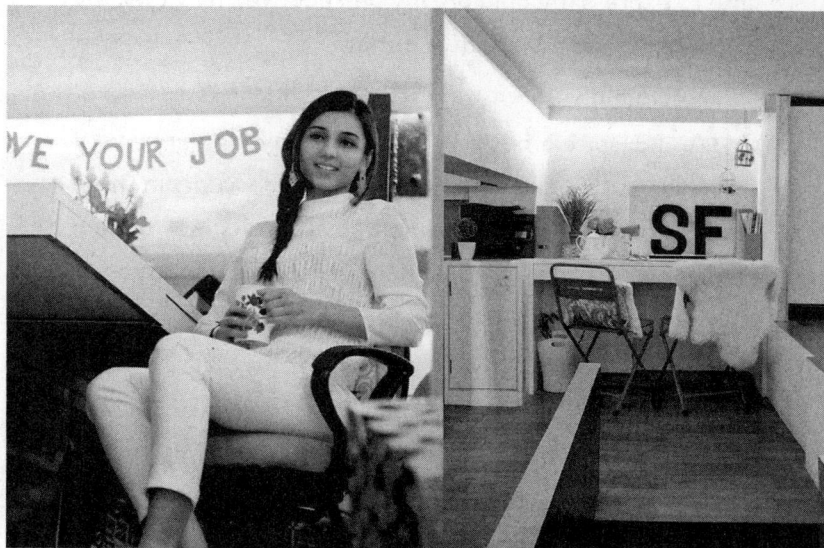

and funnily enough, I was okay with that. I wasn't aiming to be one. Until the last few years, it's safe to say my hair was never even professionally styled for any of my posts and my make-up skills were comparable to those of an eight-year-old.

A gentle reminder that these blogging days were way before the 'social media era' as we know it. Selfies, filters, face and body altering apps – these came much later.

So my blog was not so much about how great my hair or make-up looked. Contrary to popular belief, it wasn't driven to flaunt my own parade. It was a way for me to express my opinion, my perspective, my views, my outlook. It was my creative outlet.

And mind you – it was GREAT FUN.

And despite a bunch of criticism, my blog grew very quickly. At that time, having hundreds of visitors in three to four months was monumental. Curiosity was driving traffic to me. Either people were enjoying it or coming to have a good laugh. I didn't care – and it worked.

Part of a year flew by. I was getting 10,000 visits a month. It was a major milestone for me and I was thrilled. At the end of my first year of blogging, I got a collaboration request from Giorgio Armani Fragrances. In any case, back in the day, even if one email hit your inbox in three days it was an O-M-G moment. So when this email came in, I was ecstatic. Giorgio Armani was a huge deal. Influencers and creators were not recognized AT ALL in India, and the term 'influencers' didn't even exist. We went by 'bloggers' then. And this email was the very romantic beginning of my relationship with brands and collaborations.

People were noticing me, even though in commercial/professional terms, I was only being offered one perfume or one T-shirt in return for a blog post. **In those early**

days when I was just starting out, I took up all the offers that came my way. I said yes to everything. I needed to generate more content too, right? And I was always looking for any opportunity to monetize my life. Nothing was too small or irrelevant. One of my paid gigs at that time was an offshoot of my blog. The Indian team of FTV (Fashion TV) spotted my blogposts, loved my writing and hired me as a freelancer to write for their website. I was getting ₹10,000 a month for several months on that project.

GRAB OPPORTUNITIES WITH BOTH HANDS AND RUN

It helps to have blinders on at the start of a journey.

It's so easy to get swayed when we succumb to too much internal and external feedback. I'm a big believer in 'do first, think later'. Because every time I think first, I never end up doing. Especially when we're young and not so burdened with responsibilities, we should grab the experience of just 'doing', 'starting', 'implementing'.

I didn't ask five friends what they thought of me starting a blog. I asked myself the questions – and mostly always answered with a yes.

Should I start a blog?
Yes.

Should I ask a relative to help me click my pictures?
Yes.

A brand wants me to post for them for free. Should I do it?
Yes.

My advice here would be to say YES to everything! If you've got time on your hands, just take the opportunities that come knocking.

I was slowly starting to see the impact of this growth on my personality too. I was gaining my confidence back. My best friend tells me even today that learn how to accept yourself even without your job. Without your professional journey or accomplishments. But how could I? It helped me find myself. I could finally be in a room and have something of my own to say. I finally had a story to tell. It might be a blog to others, but from my POV, it was me finding myself.

Now, a few months after the Giorgio Armani perfume collaboration, the media agency that got me that 'gig' called me in for a meeting. I had been creating content for a year by then. One of the partners offered to buy out my blog and use it as a personal marketing channel for his agency's brands. Like an in-house media outlet. It was the first indication that I was on to something legitimate. Someone was willing to invest in a 'blog' I was doing for fun? They were clearly envisioning something I wasn't. Yet.

A little later, I got an email, out of the blue, from a popular lifestyle website, at the time helmed by the man who today runs one of India's largest event companies. He asked me if I was looking for a job and invited me to his office for a meeting. The address was a quaint residential building and I was so scared of going alone, I made my best friend drive me to the interview and wait downstairs until I was done. I was just about 18. He said, 'I want you to integrate your blog into my lifestyle website. You will shut down your blog and come create content for me. You'll have a secure salary to do the same thing you have been doing. You are clearly not making too much money off it right now. It's a great offer.'

Was I tempted? Well, what can I say?! I feigned interest in this meeting and left, all the while thinking to myself, 'Wow, I'm on to something!' This was the second time something like this was happening. There were two ways of looking at it: either people thought I was a threat and wanted to buy me out and shut me down. Or there was something here they could envision and I hadn't been able to see that yet. Either way, this was all the indication I needed that I was on the right track. I was now even more determined to keep my blinders on and stay on my path. **I was not going to be a supporting actor in someone else's story.**

ASK YOURSELF IF YOU CAN DO MORE

I had a captive audience who listened to me. And I had them glued to the content I was creating. Could I monetize it in another way? Ambition was gnawing at me. And I was hungry for success.

There had always been a large business mindset inculcated in me. Maybe it stemmed from my Gujarati 'business household' upbringing where transactions, deals, ambitions were dinner table conversations. My dad would always involve us in the processes of his work – show us the products, talk about his business trips and dive into details about his clients. I would sit on my mom's lap when suppliers from Rajasthan and Gujarat would be showing her their silver goods in our living room.

But how else could I monetize this business that evidently others thought was gold? Brands were not yet ready for influencer marketing, especially in India. I thought that I should perhaps have a product I could sell to my audience. I could turn my readers into customers. That would be a huge opportunity.

I started looking for wholesalers and manufacturers in India. I found multiple manufacturers, but they required large minimum order quantities. In one of my googling sprees of typing 'wholesale supplier of clothing in India', I stumbled upon a Chinese website selling the most gorgeous footwear at wholesale prices. And there were no minimum order quantities. You could order as little as ONE piece. I did the maths and I could sell these at a profit. At the time, getting fashionable footwear at an accessible price point was just not possible in India. I would post pictures (that I got from the supplier) of the shoes, style and market them through my blog, and then post it on Facebook with the prices. Each order would take two to three weeks to deliver, but I took a risk. The first pair arrived in three weeks and was gorgeous. I sold it for ₹2,000 on Facebook.

I would personally go to drop the shoes off to my customer. I was floored by the trust people had in me. I had no company registered in my name and no website. I was selling on Facebook, asking for money upfront, with a three-week delivery time. It was a blind order. But people were paying me. Trusting me.

One of the strengths in my journey (even this early on) was that I had my family looped in on every move of mine. And family never sugarcoats hard truths. When something wasn't working, my brother would point it out. When something was exceptionally nice, my mom would mention it. And this AWARENESS is key. **Whether I liked it or not, I was told the truth, shown the mirror. I was privileged to have people around me who could do it but, if you don't, you have to find a way to do it for yourself. Take note of what's working, and do more of it.**

FOCUS ON 'WHAT'S NEXT'

That's the thing about being young and wild and free. You can screw up something that's going absolutely great, but you don't take it to heart. You move on. You are agile – physically, yes, but more importantly, mentally. The same thing happens at the age of 30, and you find yourself at a therapist trying to recover from this failure. I'm proof of that. Shoes didn't work out? No problem. Let's find the next best thing that might. More googling, more deep-diving, more research.

The shoe business didn't last long because the quality was god-awful. There was no way to maintain a quality check and consistency. I called it quits before I had to deal with too many complaints.

It was around this time that I went to London for a holiday with my family. I LOVED SHOPPING THERE. H&M, Primark, Bershka, New Look – trendy, fun, high-street stuff that was accessibly priced. I would post these looks from my holiday and my audience would go absolutely crazy over them. Now, I knew I was privileged to be able to travel abroad and have access to these brands but how could I drive this same access for my readers? Fashionable, trendy items at an affordable price point. This didn't exist in India back then. How hard was that to achieve? Err, I learnt in due time.

Anyway, I ended up visiting the vintage Spitalfields market in London. I stumbled upon some gorgeous items being sold at the stalls there. Different, unique and well priced. I spent my entire shopping allowance of the trip at this amazing boutique on about 25 items by indie designers that looked cool and fashionable. These were not for me but to sell to my readers and followers. I researched pricing strategy and created a blog shop as soon as I returned to Mumbai. Setting up a blog shop was free and thanks to my coding skills, it took me no time to set up and test my model. It was a dry run. If this experiment did well, it would be a test to set up a full-blown online store. I wrote a blog about my London curation and uploaded all the information. The transaction structure was similar: order online, transfer payment in advance via bank and wait for me to ship it. All 25 items sold out in 24 hours.

I remember screaming in delight. Mind you, online shopping wasn't big then. I made a business plan and went to my family. 'I think I've hit gold. This is my second trial. It's been a success. If I have the right products, I think I can create something amazing here,' I said to them.

I started visualizing a larger game plan. I wanted to create my own e-commerce platform and build a line of products to sell. Fashionable with a mid-point price. Amazon came to India in 2013. This was a little before that. I referred to my venture as an online shop (even the word e-commerce wasn't a familiar one then). I would direct my readers to my online shop to convert them into customers and use my blog posts and images as marketing tools. I started working on the R&D.

I made a legit business plan and pitched it to my parents. I requested them to lend me some capital because even after pooling in my few blogging funds and profits from my blog shop experiments, I would need an additional amount. I would turn a profit and return it, I promised. I am really lucky that my parents had the ability by then to support me financially. Their only request to me was to gain some formal education experience in fashion as I had none. I think they were also trying to gauge if I would stick to this idea of mine. It wasn't the first idea I had had. Could this be the one that would actually make it or would I flake out? And pushing me towards education was their way of buying time. They didn't bother getting into the details and negotiations until I was sure myself.

I found a programme in London where I could do multiple short certificate courses (on branding, merchandising, styling, setting up a creative business and fashion marketing) at the London College of Fashion and Central Saint Martins. It was amazing because I already had a business idea in mind. I wasn't just studying. I was relating everything I was learning to a tangible business idea.

P.S. I also met my to-be husband Shailin on this trip, so it was doubly significant if you ask me.

After London, I went back to Mumbai and worked full time on my project.

I started with approaching local brands and telling

them about my plans. I would look up newspapers to see upcoming exhibitions, visit those exhibitions and, if I liked the brand or designer, I'd tell them I was building the 'ASOS of India' and ask if they would like to come on board. My confidence was skyrocketing but so was their confusion followed by negative responses.

I was so angry that they didn't trust my vision. See what I could see. I got so many NOs that I knew I had to reassess. Brands wouldn't come on board? No problem, I'll just create my own products and own brand.

I spent hours figuring out the products. I wasn't happy with the finishing I was finding in India at the time. The costs didn't make sense either. And most roads led to China, a big part of my early story. I had old contacts with whom I had built relationships over emails and phone calls. (Remember the shoe days?) I requested my dad to accompany me on a trip to China to explore sourcing from there. He agreed.

The next big step was to find someone to create an e-commerce website. There were all of three companies in the country at that time who knew how to build an e-commerce website. (Reminder, pre-Amazon era. Social commerce did not exist.) And the one I decided to go with – I found out later – was most definitely faking it. Two months of project delivery time turned into six months. There came a point where I would sit at their office for hours on end, sometimes even until 11 at night. My brother would accompany me to their office in the tiny by-lanes of Mumbai's busy, busy Charni Road for moral support.

The development was complex and they just couldn't get the code right. One fine day, the software developer hit a wall and just went MIA on me. I was about to launch in two days and he had ghosted me. It was stressful. There were tears.

All this while, though, my blog just never stopped. I created content while I detailed my entrepreneurial journey on my blog for my readers.

Somehow, against many odds, I launched my venture in 2012 from my living room. I vividly remember – it was my mom, my grandmom and the two interns I had hired through my blog to help with the launch. Labelling, sorting and packing products – all of it was done by this team. I kept my nose to the grindstone. I had so many goals. While my friends were travelling the world with their college mates, I found myself negotiating with delivery boys and warehouse agents to cut a good logistics deal.

By 2013, we were a profit-making company. I was selling fashion jewellery and high-street clothing at price points ranging from ₹799 to ₹2,999. Things were going well. But **when things are going good with me, I want them to get EVEN BETTER. I see the potential and I want to touch excellence.** I wanted to go big. I wanted to scale. I wanted to penetrate every household in Tier 1 India. Finding investment and the right mentor was the next logical step, and boy oh boy, was it a struggle. In 2015, I got myself an investor and we signed off on a ₹40 lakh investment. And then as I scaled this business, I saw it spiral out of my control.

KNOW THAT FAILURE IS PART OF THE PACKAGE

For more than a decade of my life, I have kept reading and rereading stories of so many people I admire – who failed before they succeeded – just for inspiration that could tide me through my failures. Bill Gates's first business venture, which analysed traffic data, failed. Mark Zuckerberg is famous for his openness to 'fall flat' and fail in order to triumph. Before Amazon became, well, Amazon, Jeff Bezos also played with a host of failed ideas – like an online auction site. As an aspiring author living in London, Huffington Post founder, journalist and author Arianna Huffington received 36 rejections for her second book.

Through the years of my e-commerce start-up, I also simultaneously dabbled in a series of small entrepreneurial ventures – again, all focused on my areas of interest. I was a serial entrepreneur even though all these attempts ended in failure. If I was passionate about an idea or saw a gap in the market, I'd just go for it. **I was never overthinking. I felt bad when I failed. But I just didn't let it set me back. You fall, you dust yourself off, you pick yourself up, and you move on. A spotless failure record is largely only held by the people who DO NOT TRY to do anything.**

I started fiddling around with a portal idea called Fashion Jobs India. In my head, it was a huge deal – the kind of portal that could potentially be acquired by LinkedIn later in life and it was able to help so many companies within the industry in their hiring process too.

My other baby was Stylehelpline.com. I envisioned it as a concierge service you could turn to for styling advice and tips on what to wear for which occasion. I also launched a separate blog called Talk Tuxedo where I keyed into men's fashion. There were no male bloggers or men's fashion content back then.

None of these ventures may have lasted very long but I kept experimenting in the fashion industry. I didn't take advice. I just went ahead and 'did it'. I realized every time I took too much advice or overanalysed, my idea got delayed.

I was mentally tuned to be overly optimistic. **I think when you're young, you're also more thick-skinned in a sense, which is why you can move on quickly. I think we become less resilient as we get older.**

I was able to deal with these failures quite quickly but the failure with e-commerce is the one that really, really hit me.

I had entered the field of e-commerce as someone committed to fashion, with an incredible knack for digital content and a digital audience. But from all the exciting stuff that I was good at, like marketing, product management and delivering high (and accessible) fashion to the Indian buyer, I was soon spending all my time on my weaknesses – operations, logistics, management and accounting. My weaknesses were now 80 per cent of the business. And I was terrible at it. But I was only one person and I was responsible for the whole 100 per cent. Well, that's the founder life. I was stressed all the time and very overworked. Soon enough, I was at breaking point.

At this point of time in life, the best gift my investor gave me was to empower me with the ability to deep dive into my accounting and finances. He taught me to look at my numbers. 'Your business is only as strong as your P&L statement,' he said. And the one thing I learnt when I studied my P&L (a profit and loss statement shows what a business's earnings and costs are) was that if I didn't wind up this business quickly I would incur heavy losses and be in deep trouble. I began to downsize the business and move it to auto-run before eventually closing it down.

The lessons I learnt while handling my unsuccessful e-commerce business (and the other failed businesses) helped me structure my future. **The most important lesson I took away: use your failures and experience to figure out what you're good at. And when you figure out what you're good at – that's what you stick to. Do what you're good at – not only what you love.**

_____

THREE

HOW TO LOVE YOURSELF

Get body confident, screw the patriarchy, be badass.

I found myself standing at the edge of 21, with a huge failure on my head.

'Wrapping up a business' might seem easy on paper but in reality, I was an emotional wreck.

The guilt was unmanageable. The shame of having to wrap up a business that was literally built IN the public eye (that was the very strength of it) was even greater.

I shut off our e-commerce operations. We had one large B2B client we continued to supply to, which helped to reduce the losses in e-commerce and aided in returning a bit of my investors' money. But there was frankly no time for self-pity or moping. I had a responsibility to my team, and I had to keep going.

I also found it hard to talk to my friends about what I was going through. It was unrelatable to them. But I was lucky to have Shailin as my sounding board. He was still studying but we spoke for hours about my business, my plans, my trajectory. In retrospect, this was the time he got the green flag. I explicitly told him how important my work was to me, and he showed up with full support, even if that meant just words of encouragement (we were in a long-distance relationship).

I had something I was good at, and that's what I instantly turned to. I amped up my old blog work, my first true love, and started on my journey as a full-time content creator and influencer in Mumbai. I am guessing this is the Masoom Minawala most of my readers are more familiar with today . . .

The idea was that if this worked out, and it proved to be a reliable business, I would earn some money and use the initial revenue to pay back my investors. That would take some pressure off me and, who knows, I could even potentially revive the e-commerce business if I wanted. That's what I told myself back then.

I divided the team and salaries between these two companies – the old venture and the new content-creation business – which made more financial sense.

Everything I learnt as an entrepreneur in e-commerce I was now applying to my content-creation business. No one else was doing that. I knew what it was like to buy inventory and hold it and not see a profit for two months. Or to invest in an app that cost the moon and not see it come to life for four months. I had learnt what it takes to build a business. I had the risk appetite, the patience and, of course, the courage. I had a financial plan and business strategy for content creation. I had salaries to pay and an investor to reimburse. I had target goals for growth for every quarter. This drive helped me grow my new business very quickly. I was willing to invest in my content in a way nobody was. I chose to work with better creative talent and production to create better videos. These things instantly set me apart from the others.

And before I knew it, the momentum was there. We had a solid content-creation business up and running.

Of course, with the success came the judgement, the discouragement. The head-shaking, the whispers of disapproval . . .

'Is she going to make a career out of *this*?'

'Does she think she is a model?'

'Aren't her thighs and hips a little too big?'

'You're not going to be able to do this without a male co-founder.'

'She can do this because she has a rich father.'

The body shaming, the sexism, the trolling. I've been mocked, ridiculed, all of it. I've walked in on people imitating me, and I don't mean it in a flattering way.

I can safely share that only two people from my entire personal circle were supportive and motivating through the early years of my career as a 'fashion' blogger. Most others (and the world at large) thought I was making an absolute fool of myself.

THERE'S NO SHAME IN YOUR BODY

Someone wise once told me this, and it stuck in my mind. It must have been during a short-lived phase of crippling anxiety (you can't blame a girl for doubting herself every so often)– caused by an off-colour Instagram comment about my body or appearance. This person said to me, 'Who do you really admire? Like, really, truly – someone who has made a genuine impact on your mind thanks to his/her contribution to you or the world at large. Did their appearance make a difference to what they did?'

When you decide to post photos of yourself on the internet for the world to view, there are a large number of people who begin to zoom in and take on the responsibility of ridiculing those photos.

I am 5 feet 2 inches tall and I have a pear-shaped body type. I think I look more like the girl next door than a glamazon with waist-length curls or a supermodel that you are used to seeing on a hoarding. I'm not a natural clotheshorse either. I have been trolled for being a certain size and height, and for having a voice that people apparently find annoying.

When you constantly see comments of strangers objectifying your body and calling parts of it deformed or too large, probably because of their emotional baggages, you subconsciously begin to believe them. **I don't know whether it's human nature or just me, but when you are repeatedly told something you begin to believe there is some truth in it. You begin to look at yourself differently in the mirror. And I hated that I was doing that.**

It was okay if my readers had a comment or criticism about my work. I would have to learn how to deal with that. But it wasn't okay that I was judged for my body, my appearance and NOT MY WORK.

When I made it to the Cannes Film Festival (you will hear how in detail in the upcoming chapters) for the second time and as one of the first few movers in this space, I was trolled for looking 'too short' on the red carpet. I did look short – there's no denying that. And no part of looking short made me ashamed or embarrassed me. I was okay with it; that was my height! How my height triggered a sea of people and their bullying at that moment bewildered me. But there was no way I could allow myself to succumb to the trolling. Perhaps people expect me to look a certain way on a red carpet (or in life, in general) but I don't have to give in to anyone else's idea of what I need to look like.

THE POWER OF SELF TALK

There's a book I clearly remember reading at the age of 16 that helped me through these moments later in life. It was *You Can Heal Your Life* by Louis Hay. It introduced me to the world of 'affirmations', a concept that would go on to shape my entire life.

It taught me the power of self-talk. **And I quickly realized that there was one voice that would need to be louder than those hundreds of hateful comments – mine.** My friends will probably still remember this – I had little Post-its stuck all over my bathroom mirror with affirmations that said:

'I love my body.'

'I am proud of my body.'

'I have a healthy body.'

'I love my curves.'

And so on . . .

I would look at myself in the mirror and say these affirmations out loud. At first, it was awkward and a bit embarrassing. With time, I enjoyed it. **With time, I let** the affirmations expand beyond the physical and they grew into other realms of my life. 'I am strong', 'I am powerful', 'I am determined', 'I am a creative genius' and so on. I had fun saying it. Today, it's my armour. I wear it to the battlefield. In moments that could break me, it's my affirmations that I turn to as second nature. It's how I lift myself up. **And I truly believe that self-talk is one of the greatest weapons we could ever possess as individuals.**

HOW TO DEAL WITH CRITICISM AND NEGATIVITY

While I was, after trying really hard and working on myself, able to beat the body shaming and physical criticism, what I went on to struggle with was the attacks on my choice of career, the catty comments on the frivolousness of my job and the criticism for being privileged.

Many of the comments actually amplified and exposed genuine weaknesses of mine. When your legs shake thinking about how you will manage to build a career out of taking photos and then you hear more than a dozen people ridiculing that very same idea, your inner fears get confirmed. How do you shut them out when you too are having the same doubts?

Comments around privilege

████████ 28w

Can you make one post where you aren't glorifying yourself. Nope

6 likes   Reply

████████ 36w

Everything is easy when you have crores in your pockets and you don't have to put food on the table by choice. Congratulations though. Everything you have achieved is commendable

8 likes   Reply

████████ 5w

Come on ! Atleast show the correct picture. Show that you are travelling with a Nanny who full time takes care of the child while you are able to work and travel. Such pictures are so delusional and we mothers know how things truly work. You can't do it alone, so might as well show the true picture!

67 likes   Reply

████████ 36w

Not another video by this lady showing off about working and being a mother!! C'mon, for generations now our mothers and grandmothers have been doing it and till today you see roadside workers tying their kids to their backs and working.. they don't have underpaid or unpaid assistants like you have to help them 😐 also next time you are travelling you might want to focus more on loading the bags in the trolley properly first before posing

79 likes   Reply

39w
Undisclosed sponsorships, blatant lying for money when she's already THAT rich, at least be authentic to your work!!!! I'm pretty darn sure she received the sunscreen few days ago and here she's all i use it regularly everyday woah i feel bad for the people following her

2 likes   Reply

54w
So sad that you need to dance in reels while pregnant and worry so much about content and social media! Seriously what's wrong with these influencers people... keep making cringe reels and dancing with big belly... cheez learn to enjoy your life away from social media

4 likes   Reply

60w
And don't forget you had your father's money to back you up😅

Reply

56w
Is there any lack of confidence at if you will stay away from social media your followers will go.. and passed your posted such a good content and now it's getting very cringy and boring..one time two time theek h not every now and then on my feed same thing..

18 likes   Reply

56w
Sirf Naam hi masoom hae

1 like   Reply   See Translation

████████ 100w

Constantly blowing your own trumpet. Tiring man
tiring! Not a thing to learn on this page.

9 likes   Reply

████████ 58w

What is the peak of career this masoom is talking
about? Iska career peak tab se hi shuru ho gya tha
jab se yeh paida hui thi. Bro tu dance karti hai reels
pe, mars pe mission nhi send kar rhi.

Reply   See Translation

████████ 59w

Loll your dad is a diamond merchant , you never had
to worry about money. You have people who will
take care of things for you

182 likes   Reply

████████ 95w

It's so sad that because of the wealth disparity
people that lack creativity get exposure simply due
to having plenty of funds to use. This post exposes
that. You look bad and uncool. In the end, your
money will not rescue your bad taste. Vain and
uncultured.

4 likes   Reply

████████ 59w

@shehrygetsready facts LOL. She's always
acting like she's the ONLY women who goes
through things and has to attach
empowerment to everything she does. She
literally had a golden spoon in her mouth the
day she was born.

43 likes   Reply

> **Pray Serve Love** ▓▓▓▓▓ 42w
> Of course you can do coming from a diamond merchant millionaire family . Generational wealth people talking about struggles...
> 4 likes   Reply

> ▓▓▓▓▓ 58w
> @masoomsharmaofficial This isn't empowering you privilege chick see a labour carrying her kid to work
> 4 likes   Reply

> ▓▓▓▓▓ 56w
> You are trying too hard to look cool in social media 😊
> 106 likes   Reply

I hate to play the damsel in distress, so I have to admit that in my career trajectory there have been some glaring mistakes that I too have committed – through my content, my communication or my lack of awareness. I've been called out on it by faceless accounts, often with abusive comments, mostly always with personal attacks and commentary that can quite honestly strip a person of any visible mental balance. I learnt then that this was a part of the job. If I had chosen to have a job that was in the public eye, I needed to be more responsible with my words and actions. Or simply deal with the repercussions.

If I wanted to have a job that required projecting 'externally' to thousands of people, there would have to be A LOT of work I needed to put in internally.

It could start with just one comment. Steadily increase to a few. Rapidly increase to 50. People would start sharing stories about it. I would start getting screenshots from friends and family to check if I'm aware of these shares. Media outlets and publications would pick it up for fodder. (We all know how well a takedown performs from a clickbait POV.) And it would turn into a full-blown PR debacle on the internet and a full-blown anxiety attack in my head.

Encountering trolls

Follow   X

Also married to a Gem merchant. People not acknowledging their privilege and giving life lessons to mere mortals is probably the most annoying thing on SM these days. Mostly by influencers.

4:47 PM · Oct 12, 2022

174d

So pretentious. The accent, the demeanour everything. WannabeMinawala

The hard life of Masoom Minawala

`From Instagram`

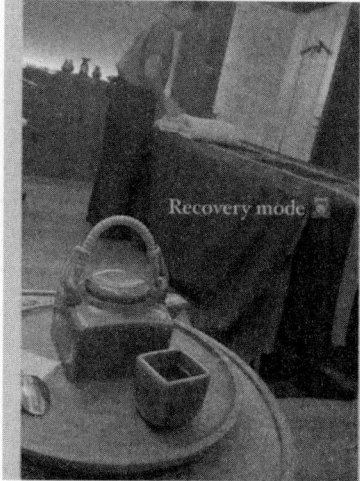

Recovery mode

I don't even understand how she landed Estee Lauder. She's all over the ads & banners.

12/10/2022

I not only want @MasoomMinawala daddy's money but also confidence to say that I'm an entrepreneur who has started her career from scratch. 'passion into business'

💬   ↻ 2   ♡ 17   ılıl   🔖   ⬆

174d

One of the worse 😂 I and my friend emailed her in 2020 about her dumb teenage accent. And now after 3 years she is back with this BS. So yesterday I have again sent her DM that plewse stop talking like a teenage dumb girl.

Masooooom why???? Clownette

1d

Replying to @MasoomMinawala and

That you are yet another attention seeking little snowflake?

💬   🔁   ♡   📊 5   🔖   ⬆️

· 09/09/2023

when I tell you **masoom minawala** has literally never uplifted me...

💬   🔁   ♡ 2   📊 556   🔖   ⬆️

No matter what, I was never really able to get behind Masoom. Seems super shady behind all that toxic positivity she portrays.

Masoom is like a snake with the face of squirrel.

I still wonder how people fell in her trap of preaching.

███████████████████ 09/09/2023 ···

Replying to ████████████████

Like **Masoom Minawala** girl you're a millionaire and you're not stuck at some soul sucking desk job. NOW YOU WANT A PADMA SHRI TOO?!?

💬   🔁   ♡   ılıl 512   🔖   ⬆

████████████

Insider

SOBO meets desi just moved to Europe accent

I have been through a phase when just hearing the word 'troll' has caused me anxiety. That terrible, icky feeling in the stomach ... yes ... that. I would receive one negative comment on my content and my thoughts would spiral out of control. The comments could be an attack or a disagreement. Should I delete the offending post that triggered the hate? Should I delete the hateful comment? Should I report the account? Screenshots would go to my team, my best friend, maybe my family. I could be in the middle of a conference call or a shoot and I would drop everything and focus on this one comment and what I had to do to stop this from nosediving into a full-blown trolling episode. And, let me add, this is ONE negative comment among 200 positive, motivating, unbelievably encouraging ones.

I felt sick for allowing somebody I didn't know to have this kind of control over me. I wasn't even able to process the situation because I was simply consumed with fear. The fear of being cancelled and losing the job I love so much. In my defence, I had seen it happen. I had seen influencers being 'cancelled' and never showing up on the internet again. I knew I couldn't go on like this . . .

Whenever I would discuss my insecurities with my friends or family, I was met with stock responses. 'Why do you care about what people say?' These responses didn't make sense to me. They weren't being personally attacked on public platforms for everyone to read! I felt no one understood me or my industry and where I was coming from. 'It's a part and parcel of your job,' they'd say. But I was suffering from anxiety. What my family and friends were trying to say may not have been wrong but I probably didn't want to hear it or it wasn't being conveyed to me in the right way.

I knew I had to find a way out of this. I loved my job way too much. And if I didn't find a way to deal with this, screw the trolls but I didn't know how much longer my mental health could continue in this occupation. I turned to professional help via a life coach who helped me slowly and steadily weave through this process.

Back in the day, I loved playing the victim card. 'Oh, these trolls – what do they think? They can hide behind a faceless account and say what they want to me?' But I quickly learnt this might not be the best solution. Attack isn't always the best defence.

Among other things, **my life coach, Saloni Suri, taught me to ask myself this question after every 'incident' – 'What can you learn from this situation?' And that shift in perspective has helped me sail through a good many storms.**

Here are some solutions that worked for me. I say this after having used all these tools – it can work for you too, no matter what field or stage of life you are in.

1. **ACCEPT:** No matter what you say or do, people will have an opinion. In the working world, criticism can be invalid (in which case, happily ignore it) or valid. **Valid criticism from credible sources can be tapped for self-improvement and eventually for success.** A good example here would be the time I did a video on my luxury handbag collection and received a ton of terrible feedback. I thought, 'Why am I being trolled when international influencers do stuff like this all the time? I've worked very hard to

buy these handbags.' Turns out, the content wasn't the problem. It was the timing and the narrative. It was the way I presented the content. It was a few months after Covid hit and people weren't in the mood for conspicuous luxury consumption. My caption said 'If you want the bags, you must work hard for it', and coming from someone whose life was cushioned against hardship when millions were on the brink of it, it was the wrong communication at the wrong time. The fact is, I am privileged, way more so than most people, and that's something I have learnt to accept and be upfront about. The onus is on me to be more sensitive to every background.

2. **COURSE CORRECT:** It doesn't make you a smaller person. I once posted a video debating another influencer's post mocking what influencers do and how trivial our job is. His post had angered me and I retaliated via a post that spoke about the layers of impact influencers have had. Towards the end of the video, I drew comparisons to other professions, including doctors, scientists and engineers, which, in retrospect, wasn't a fair analogy. Recognizing this, I took full responsibility

for the lapse in my expression and promptly apologized to my community. I clarified that my aim was never to diminish anyone or compare the importance of various professions. Even after my luxury handbag video fiasco, I apologized to my community for being insensitive. I am acutely conscious now. A fellow creator advised me that sometimes the simplest solution is telling your community that you hear them, and that you will try and do better for them. This is a simple, game-changing lesson. **Everyone makes mistakes and sometimes just having the courage to own up to those mistakes and being accountable is the simplest and most graceful route.**

3. **IGNORE:** It's key to know when it's a valid criticism and when it's not. And when it's invalid, I simply reduce the background noise. **Ignore the bullies. Press mute. Don't engage with the 'trolls' in real life or online.** My favourite trick is to imagine myself walking with a glass bubble around me and the invalid criticism or unnecessary shaming coming my way is simply hitting the glass bubble and bouncing back. I do not give it permission to pierce my energy.

4. **PRIORITIZE THE POSITIVE: Every time I paid attention to one negative comment, I was being unfair to the 100 positive ones.** That's not something I wanted with my life. This holds true for all of us, at any stage of our lives or careers.

5. **BE YOURSELF: Draw that line and stick to your guns when needed.** This comes with learning to be a leader. Stop seeking the world's approval. You cannot please everyone, this much is true. I would much rather just please myself, right? You don't like what I'm wearing? That's okay, I like it. You don't like what I'm saying? That's okay, I'm allowed to have a perspective that's different from yours.

USE EVERY MISTAKE TO RECALIBRATE

It's easy to play victim when 'cancel culture' is a buzzword. But the fact of the matter is, I have made mistakes. So many.

What the reaction to those mistakes has been is frankly out of my control, but the action itself, the mistake itself, is wholly and solely my responsibility.

Everyone makes mistakes. Personally and

professionally, they are the key to growth. But it's so hard to convince yourself of that while living the mistake itself. Is there any professional who has had a perfect run? I doubt it.

But I couldn't wrap my head around the fact that each professional mistake I made was going to play out so publicly. Everyone could see my errors. People around the world could view it, criticize it, comment on it and pass judgement. This just tormented me.

It also took a lot of therapy for me to realize that I was never going to stop making mistakes. So I had to find a way to deal with them. It didn't hurt to know, as I mentioned above, that sometimes the most graceful way to deal with a mistake is to **put your hand up and say 'mea culpa'. Acknowledge and apologize – always.**

There was a time when I promoted a bag that was an Indian label's rip-off of a large international luxury house's design. I was called out publicly by my audience and privately by said luxury brand, which was also one of my most important clients.

Another time, I was promoting Indian craft for one of the IPs we created called #IndiaILove while wearing a digital print of Bandhani! I didn't realize it was a digital print and thought it was the real thing. Here I was promoting craft while flaunting the very technology that was putting craftspeople out of business.

I once mispronounced the name of one of India's greatest monuments on a live stream.

There have been multiple incidents where I've not been conscious of the privilege and cushioning I come from and I've been ignorant of the fact that audiences watching that content might not come from a similar place of privilege.

And in all of these, I've felt terrible beyond explanation.

Sometimes the backlash has been so intense on my mistakes that it has been hard to move on. In that moment, it's so hard to remind myself that **yes, the wins and the victories are important, but the mistakes are just as important in this journey of life. And sometimes, they even teach us more than the wins do.**

It's something my life coach had said to me: **'It's not about how hard you fall but how fast you get up.' Every time I fall, I learn to get up and keep running – faster. The falls will never stop. But I will keep getting up.**

SCREW THE PATRIARCHY

As a woman, there will always be someone telling you that you can't do it.

When I launched my e-commerce venture, the industry was creating waves the world over but in India, we were one of the very first few. The toughest part was the gender discrimination I faced. I was constantly undermined and undervalued as a female entrepreneur. This might be slightly unrelatable in 2024, but in 2015, it was a proper roadblock. It was pointed out to me every step of the way. My marketing costs plus customer acquisition costs were negligible because I was driving customers from my blog. So, if you ask me, it was a rock-solid business idea with a rock-solid trajectory (at that time at least, before things went belly up). And I was not the only one to think so. I started getting offers from investors and big, reputed, celebrated funds at that. And I did need more expertise, more capital. Investors were ruthless and I knew I had to bring my A-Game if I wanted to drive it to a 100-crore company like I hoped to.

I actively started pursuing the funding conversation and doing investor meetings. They always started well. I knew how to make a bulletproof pitch, and my passion was obvious. What shook me though is how these meetings always wound up. It was never about the business or what I hoped to build it into. It was always about my gender.

'You need to get a male co-founder if you want to scale this business.'

'It's not a solid business idea because you're a young, unmarried girl. You'll quit when you get married.'

'Is your dad around? Someone who can help me with more details on the finances.'

'What will happen to the business once you have kids?'

I wasn't enough for them. When more powerful, more experienced, more seasoned individuals are all expressing the same worry – you are not enough because you're a girl – you don't think it's rigged; you tend to start believing them. And their bullshit.

These moments come for all of us. Where you fall for this trap and lose the motivation, the drive, the eagerness. Because at some point it gets boring to keep fighting. It gets tiring when nobody seems to be listening.

But you know what turned it around for me? Ironically, it was the men I was privileged enough to come home to. My husband, my father, my brother, my grandfather.

When I would return home to my family, feeling dejected and rejected, they would tell me that what I had just heard was NOT true. They would tell me to believe in myself. They would not let me write my story based on sexist judgements. And they would keep telling me until I believed them.

PRO TIP: CHOOSE WHO YOU LISTEN TO

When you find yourself in an uncomfortable situation –
especially when someone has the audacity to define you
or your story through their lens – go to someone you
trust, who has your best interests at heart, and ask them
what they think. Let them rewrite the story for you. And
that's the only version you are allowed to tell yourself.
For, what you tell yourself is what becomes your reality.

In hindsight, it didn't matter what these people
thought of me. They clearly weren't the type I needed
to please. **If I had to prove to my investors that a woman
was as good as a man in business, they weren't the right
investors for me.**

Want more of a sneak peek into the constant
commentary borne by a working woman? I'm sure many
of the women reading this have had versions of this
happen to them. Well, you are not alone.

'It's great that you have some timepass to do to
keep yourself busy.' Well, do men go to work 'to keep
themselves busy'?

A family member once said in Gujarati, 'Chokrao aave tya sudhi aa bau saaru timepass che.' This translates to: 'This is a great pastime until you have kids.' I remember going into my room and crying after that one. Yes, you can call me weak for that, but crying is my way of expressing my anger and I'm proud of it. This comment came after having proven myself multiple times on global platforms. I can't even imagine what it must be like for someone who is still trying to start out, to make things work for themselves or simply just working hard at any career.

I am not confrontational by nature. But these situations were arising so often that I felt I had to do something about it. I couldn't shy away from it. I felt like I should take a stand for the women around me. **Like, I was being called out for having a 'rich father' and later a 'rich husband'. It was presumptuous. No one called out my husband for having a 'rich wife' or my father for having a 'rich daughter'.** Whether people like it or not, I do contribute to my father's and brother and sister-in-law's businesses today via my community of followers by promoting their businesses and driving to them a relevant number of sales; and my marriage is an equal relationship in every way, including financially.

I saw some pretty ugly demons of patriarchy after marriage too. There was sexism dripping in everyday life and speech, in the most mundane of tasks. I could not believe how many women were facing this and how many of these comments came from women themselves.

'I have so much respect for your husband for allowing you to continue in this field.'

'Is your husband okay with you travelling so much for work?'

'You're leaving your husband and going on another work trip?'

Well, Shailin and I both travel equally for work. No one ever asked him, 'You're leaving your wife and going on a work trip?'

Sexism, in so many ways, has infiltrated my professional and personal life. 'You should do this only till you have a child.' Now that's a scary thought. My husband and I both contribute equally to our household and our lives, more so now that our family is expanding. If one of us didn't work, we may not have the life we aspire to for our family.

I now try and create women-focused content (including the book in your hands!) because I wish I had had that support back then. I am a huge advocate for women in business because I was never 'given a seat at the table' so to speak. My past negative experiences in handling finances and naysayers was one of the primary reasons I launched a vertical called Empowher in 2022. It is an initiative to converse, build and elevate women-led businesses and professions. I wanted to support other women who might have been going through similar situations as I had. I wanted to create a space where women could come together, learn from each other and lift each other up.

Women in my Empowher community have started taking larger steps towards their financial independence. And they're having tough conversations with the men in their lives about it. It was a big achievement for me and gave me a huge feeling of fulfilment.

MY BOX OF ADVICE TO YOUNG WOMEN — THE PREACHY KIND

1. Just because someone thinks your gender is your weakness does not make it true. Your gender is your strength. Believe it.

2. We have years of patriarchal conditioning to beat; it's not an overnight process, and it's sure as hell not going to happen through one heated confrontation. It takes patience and consistency to change the narrative.

3. Our actions and our victories will bring about more changes than our words will.

4. Don't let others decide how fast or slow, or close or far you should go in your career.

MY BOX OF ADVICE TO YOUNG WOMEN — THE LIFE-CHANGING KIND

1. Save a percentage of your income and invest it. Don't be overwhelmed by these financial terms. Ask five people in your inner circle to guide you and you will have answers before you know it.

2. Walk away from people and situations that make you feel less about yourself.

3. Develop a strong support network of people who will lift you up. We are social animals – a person is not an island. Ask for help.

—————

FOUR

#GETSHITDONE

When it comes to success in any profession, an MBA is optional. Earning a GSD (Get Shit Done) is mandatory.

'If you had an MBA, things would have been different.' Ever heard that? God knows I have.

But **if there is one thing I have learnt, it is this: when it comes to succeeding in your entrepreneurial or professional journey, or in your life, the only limits you have are the ones you set for yourself, which means you can work through everything as long as you #justGSD.**

After my e-commerce venture went south, I started off as a full-time content creator and influencer in Mumbai with a small community of online followers backing me. I tested the waters slowly. I pursued it and got tons of collaborations and started building new relationships for work. A few months later, in February 2017, I got married to my long-term boyfriend Shailin who lived in Belgium at the time. My wedding went viral. It was the first 'influencer' wedding that went heavily online and the idea of a virtual wedding actually came about from the intention of having a new content format. My wedding was a huge boost to my business.

After my wedding, I didn't get my residency visa for Belgium right away so I stayed back home for six months. That gave me a lot of time in Mumbai to work on content creation as my full-time business.

I found top-of-the-rung clients quickly, names such as Estée Lauder, Longchamp, Jo Malone, Garnier and Samsung, among others. I was able to give my community a product – i.e. my content – that I was so damn proud of. I would get emails from brands and agencies with collaboration requests that would lead to lengthy exchanges and even carry on to multiple phone calls – all of which I addressed myself. My phone was ringing off the hook. Agencies wanted to send in gifts, brands wanted to understand how collaborations work, founders wanted to negotiate. I was working non-stop. The coordination was intense, work was booming and opportunities were immense.

My e-commerce team began to support me more and more as the demand grew. Even though it had been about seven years since I first started, the industry hadn't gained so many entrants. But the readers, the audience, the fans – that sector had expanded immensely. Everyone knew what a 'content creator' and 'influencer' was by this time.

They understood it, they ridiculed it, but they were so damn addicted to it.

I had been waiting for this very moment. Until this time, I was bending over backwards to get a brand to invest a few thousand in me and my work but now it was time to reap the rewards for the work I had put in. I mustered up the courage and increased my prices.

After two long years of work stress, discrepancies in accounting and investor woes in e-commerce, I had one year where I felt successful and abundant. I started to gain a firm foothold in the fashion and luxury spaces in India. All of a sudden, I was on the cover of a magazine, featured in the pages of *Vogue* and *Elle*, and in CNN's 20 under 40 list.

But I felt like I had barely tasted the upward curve of this roller coaster before I had to move to Belgium.

As soon as I moved, there was a drastic drop in business. I stopped receiving event invites (obviously, I wasn't in the country) but I also stopped receiving press releases, product launch announcements and collaboration requests trickled down to a mere 20 per cent. Things had crashed, again. All the relationships I had just solidified with Indian PR companies and brands came to nothing. I was basically kicked off all the PR lists.

I spoke to acquaintances in the industry, and they said it was assumed I wouldn't continue my career now that I was married and had moved countries. Wow.

Additionally, at that time, building commercial relationships with brands was about receiving free PR 'gift' packages and creating content about those products. That's how brands would see your abilities and creativity and decide to invest in you. Logistically, given my distance from India, I was no longer a cost-efficient recipient for them. Why would Indian brands or the India offices of international brands send me a package in Belgium when they could send it to another influencer sitting in India?

I mulled over the situation in front of me and applied **rule no. 1 of GSD.**

DON'T EVER WALLOW IN SELF-PITY

You assess the situation and play the card that's dealt in your favour.

I wasn't in India any more and that was negatively affecting my business. But I was in a new country . . . maybe that's a route that could prove to be more successful?

Belgium is a beautiful country with some iconic fashion industry veterans hailing from there: Dries van Noten, Raf Simons, Olivier Theyskens. But it was also one with an ageing population and low internet consumption.

My team and I worked on an Excel sheet after a lot of research on Google and social media for relevant contacts. I then started to reach out to PR companies based in Belgium.

I'd get responses from local PR companies a good few weeks after I wrote to them. And some wouldn't reply at all. Meetings just wouldn't work out. For the handful that worked out, they asked me how much of my audience was Belgian and I had to embarrassingly look away. I asked the Indian counterparts of various international brands to connect me to their European teams so I could continue my working relationship with them, but there was literally no follow-up or interest. It was a global mandate that Indian talent would be coordinated by the Indian team only.

There's one major lesson I've learnt in my career and it's a very hard reality that, at any point of time in life, you can lose everything you've achieved till then. Success doesn't come with a warranty. Over my career trajectory, I have had ups and downs multiple times and unfortunately when you're down, you have to be your own ladder.

My business was taking a major hit but on the personal front I had begun to blossom. Somehow, having a blank slate allowed me the freedom of redefining myself. I was no longer in an environment where I had old labels attached to me. Everything was a first impression and I found that I could choose to be whoever I wanted to be. I chose to be more accepting (I was picking that up from my husband), I chose to be more outgoing (I needed the Mumbai energy) and I chose to be vulnerable with new relationships (I sorely missed the comfort of my family).

I began to love this new version of me. And when you begin to love yourself, magic happens.

Anyway, I soon noticed a spate of Indian and Indian-origin influencers in the UK. A deep dive made me realize that it was because of the Indian diaspora in the UK – which was only growing in size and strength. 'I could potentially explore this market,' I thought. It was a two-hour train ride away and, unlike in Belgium, I actually had an audience that resided in the UK. I thought the large Indian and South Asian diaspora of the UK would find my content relatable. I needed to crack the European brand market. That was my focus and goal. I dreamt of working with Louis Vuitton, L'Oréal and the H&Ms of the world, with them paying me to create content around their products.

I repeated the PR company exercise. First, I researched who the leading ones were in my category and then I reached out to them, explaining what I do, and sent them samples of my past work. I saw a difference already – there were 5x the PR companies in the UK compared to Belgium. I started getting responses and began to set up meetings.

Enter rule no. 2 of getting shit done.

DO IT YOURSELF

It was much easier to correspond over email and keep it at that rather than travelling to a different country and investing in hotels and tickets. But showing up for a face-to-face meeting convinced people I was really invested. **People might forget an email, but they probably will not forget an hour-long one-on-one**. This rule has stood me in good stead, and it can for you too. Remember, face-to-face time is invaluable, no matter what your profession.

If you have the chance to physically meet people

who are important for your career, grab it. Make these opportunities happen. Show up at networking events, for instance. Because when an opportunity arises, and people need to think of who to give the contract/gig to, they'll think of you if they can put a face to a name. But they're unlikely to remember your email. Also, so much of tone and nuance is lost over an email. It lends itself to cut-and-dried decisions and communication. In the world of remote working, a face-to-face meeting (even over Zoom) can make work happen better, quicker and happier. People will understand you better. They'll see your magic!

Coming back to my story, during my first work trip to London, I initiated some meetings. The first thing they asked me is where I lived. Now, I actually lived between Belgium and India. But I couldn't say that.

So here is rule no. 3 of GSD.

FAKE IT TILL YOU MAKE IT

You might not be there yet – but pretending like you are is half the battle won.

Where do I live? I wasn't expecting this question at all. I had already explained in my introductory emails that

I had a percentage of my audience residing in the UK along with screenshots of my audience break-up. Well, my strategy was faking it. And pretending that I lived in London. I needed to say that to get paid deals in the UK.

Now that I was faking 'living' in London, that lie also needed a ton of evidence to back it up. I was lucky and privileged that I could afford to take day trips to London from Belgium and do shoots there so people would see the background of London in my content and my UK audience would grow. Day trips were exhausting because I would take a 6 a.m. train out and then a 7 p.m. train back and spend the day shooting (all the while lugging a huge suitcase around with the items I would shoot with) and doing meetings. But at least this way I didn't have to spend on a hotel and I could save that cost. I may have been totally exhausted but, hey, I was blessed and lucky to have the opportunity to make this life for myself.

With this situation, agencies also wanted an address in London to deliver packages to. Since this package topic keeps coming up, let me explain in detail . . . Packages are a pivotal part of the content-creation business. Especially in the fashion and lifestyle space. The very foundation of the business is based on using products and recommending them to your community. So the beginning of that chain requires brands and agencies to send products to said creators – as gifts, as barters, as a way to experience and touch and feel their product, introduce a new launch and so on.

I asked one of Shailin's university friends who lived in London if I could share his address with agencies as my address. He gracefully agreed but, with time, the packages got so frequent, I knew it was an extreme inconvenience for him. I then got a PO box in London (just one of those #GSD moments). I made more and more trips, sometimes on a weekly basis. I even had a local manager. Even while I'd be in Belgium with my husband, I never disclosed my location on social media. I would post like I was in the UK.

And that is golden GSD rule no. 4.

QUIT OVERTHINKING

Give situations a chance without overthinking the consequences. You never know which step could turn into an entire road.

On a side note, I had one important realization not too long ago – that it was far easier to 'GSD' in the beginning. Why? Well, for one, as I've said before, **there was less 'overthinking' involved** because I was young, naïve and a blank slate. I had fewer layers. I cared less. I had less to lose. Whenever I thought of doing something new (and I was quite a serial entrepreneur) – a large business, a small project or even simply reaching out to someone – it required less energy because I wasn't focused on consequences. But, it took me months to convince myself I am even worthy of having my name on the cover of a book. **I just wanted to get shit done and not focus on the hundred 'what ifs' that life throws at you.**

In this period, I was working with brands like BOOTS, Sephora, Aspinal of London, Estée Lauder, Bobbi Brown and more. A cold email turned into a meeting and I had the brand partnerships I was eagerly on the hunt for. There were few but at least they were there.

By doing what I had to do to get through the door, I did get through the door, but, in a few months, I was physically and mentally exhausted. I was shuffling between two countries, neither of which felt like home to me. My followers weren't growing in numbers globally, or in the UK, even though my engagement was high. And that brings us to roadblock number five hundred and sixty-three. This whole plan was based on a pretence – and a pretence only takes you so far. I was learning that for the first time.

Instead of fussing about why I wasn't growing, I just hired a data analytics consultant to help me figure things out.

I knew the power of data from my e-commerce days and even though this was an unconventional practice in the influencer industry (and hella expensive), I thought it might give me some strategic guidance. Her report and analysis said that my primary engagement was still from my India-based followers. My audience growth had expanded to the Indian diaspora all around the world but 70 per cent was still coming from India. When I found myself in a different country, I thought my original audience wouldn't relate to me. But I was wrong. Ever since that time, reading and analysing data has become a strong arm of our strategy. And this defines my business even today. We do it on a daily basis. It is how my brand drives that crazy conversion rate. A conversion rate in my business is the proportion of the number of people who view a post and then follow through on the action being nudged – whether it's clicking a link or purchasing a product.

A FRIEND WHO DOESN'T LIE TO MAKE YOU FEEL BETTER

Anyone can see how far they've come using data. Data doesn't lie and it tells the harsh truth pretty succinctly. It's simple. You want to see how much you procrastinate through the day – look at your phone's usage hours. You want to see how much you spend – log your expenses. If you feel you are stagnating in your career – look at your income growth and compare it to the industry average. Data can tell you many of the awful hard truths that your friends and loved ones may not for fear of hurting you.

I now saw an opportunity there, which I didn't think was possible before. I thought I should focus on my Indian community and my original market. The primary limitation – i.e. location and distance – maybe was just in my head. Maybe I could find a way around it.

That little light just flicked on!

And this progresses naturally into GSD rule no. 5.

TAKE A RISK ON YOURSELF

What did I then do? I shut down all the barriers I had made up in my head and forced myself to go back to that seed that was first sown. Back to why I started this. Back to that 18-year-old sitting on her canopy bed and coding at 3 a.m. It was my love for fashion. My love for having a unique perspective and being able to share it with my community and the world. I asked myself how I could marry that passion with what my circumstances were today. Could I be the link for my Indian followers to the global fashion scene? Could I use the fact that I was living in Europe to my advantage and create content in unique backgrounds but do it with Indian designers? Could I be the bridge between the Indian and European fashion industries?

But I knew this was a concept I would have to first test drive myself before roping in the collaborations. I curated and chose looks from Indian designers and told them I would take care of the logistics and shipping back and forth from Belgium. I would then take a day trip by train from Antwerp to Paris to shoot in an embroidered lehenga outside the Eiffel Tower or in a cocktail saree at La Grand-Place in Brussels.

My audience absolutely loved this content.

Since the route of PR agencies in Belgium or the UK wasn't very fruitful, I turned back to my Indian relationships – both with Indian designers and also with the India offices of international brands. This time it was with a different proposal keeping my new strategy in mind.

I told them I wasn't interested in receiving their gifts or packages at all. I was ready for the next step . . . I wanted to be the Indian representative that would attend all their key global events – product launches, fashion weeks, press trips, special events, etc., on behalf of India. I wanted to do something larger with them. I wanted to be their global brand ambassador and spokesperson. And I was ready to invest the time and energy it would take to build this until I got there. And they recognized this as hunger, as ambition (which it rightly was). I was asking for something nobody else was, and they loved it.

The more I focused on being the link between the global fashion industry and India, the more I realized how enormous its impact could be. I kept digging and the gaps were glaring.

I would see magnificent international brand events globally like Bvlgari, Louis Vuitton and Chopard with representatives from around the world; and I wondered why there was nobody from India.

Let's just crunch some numbers to understand my thought process. When I started off around 2017, India's luxury market was set to grow from USD 23.8 billion to about USD 30 billion by the end of 2018 going into 2019. That's the kind of growth potential I fathomed. And I think I read the signs right. To fast forward to *today*, incidentally, as per a report by global consulting firm Bain & Company released towards the end of 2023, India's luxury market is set to expand by 3.5 times its current size and reach a cool USD 200 billion by 2030.

Anyway, going back to the story: I would turn to the India-based brand reps of global behemoths and ask them why there was no representative from India. They would look at me blankly. The India team at times wouldn't even know about many of the most important events their global headquarters were hosting, where influencers from other countries were being invited. I told them, let's not wait for global teams to alert you before events; let's reach out to them now itself and inform them that one of your key representatives (me) resided in Europe and would like to participate in any events or shows happening in the region.

You might think it was far-fetched but I'm a living example of being pushy and audacious to get what you want. They did it. And it worked. You see, globally everyone wanted a piece of India but, in their heads, they just found it too far, too inaccessible.

This wasn't the Masoom Minawala story any more. It was the India story. And the more I started living the India story, the more obsessed I got with it.

Slowly and steadily, international fashion weeks and global events became an important arm of this new strategy and they helped me utilize my proximity to global fashion capitals and being in Europe to its fullest advantage. And my audience was transfixed – somehow me being at events held in London or Paris of British or French designers (some of which were not even famously known brand names) seemed to validate my work. My followers liked seeing me at international fashion weeks, store openings, product launches and film festivals. It gave me credibility. It was also unique and fresh content. Which other girl from Prabhadevi was at fashion shows in London or Paris? The more I did it, the more global brand events I got invited to.

My proximity to Europe and the UK helped as the brands didn't need to fly in someone who appealed to the Indian market from India. Win-win, right?

Now, like any young woman with even the tiniest

inclination towards fashion, Paris Fashion Week was a dream for me. The fashion week calendar is officially published online two weeks before the shows. In 2018 (year one of living in Belgium), after the calendar was published, I sat up like a hawk for eight hours looking for PR representatives and contacts through Instagram and LinkedIn. I then reached out to them introducing myself and my work. I spent days sending emails. I had a response from only *one* designer, who I hadn't even heard of.

What would I go and do with just one invite, I thought. But my husband insisted I go. 'Paris is so close,' he said. 'If you don't push yourself out of your comfort zone, how will you make it?' I booked the 6 a.m. train from Antwerp to Paris with two suitcases filled with clothes, shoes and bags and the hope that this would help me take my business to the next level. Anyway, it wasn't even a show. It was a presentation (presentations are like temporary art galleries where designers stage a live installation of their latest pieces and the attendees take their own time to touch, feel and critique the collection).

I put up a post saying I was going and asking who else was around. A childhood friend of mine, who is now a reputed jewellery designer, said she was going to be there. I asked her if she had any show passes or contacts who could help me get my foot in the door. Chances were slim as invites went out well in advance. Well, as luck would have it, she told me about a fairly large Manish Arora show that she had a ticket for but wasn't going to go to herself. I now had a ticket.

On to GSD rule no. 6.

NO SHOWING UP = NO OPTIONS

I sauntered into my first fashion show in Paris, thanks to my friend's generosity and my willingness to ASK, made small talk and exchanged phone numbers. I waited at the venue for 45 minutes after the show ended, hoping a photographer would come up to me and take photos of my look. A stranger who happened to be a micro European magazine's stylist struck up a conversation with me and I told her it was my first time. She explained to me how a fashion week works . . . how photographers have the entire schedule and locations of the shows (they've been coming for multiple seasons so they build a close-knit community that shares information) and run from one venue to the other to catch good photo ops of celebrities and influencers, which in turn they sell to publications.

THE PRIYANKA CHOPRA MODEL

I have been completely inspired by something I once heard from the managing director of a top Mumbai-based brand solutions company. And it was about a mega global icon whom I truly admire. Priyanka Chopra. **The managing director told me that when Priyanka Chopra moved out of Bollywood to the Los Angeles and New York circle, she cracked the space by making her presence felt everywhere. She was willing to take a 12-hour flight to be seen at the right place at the right time and then another 12-hour flight back to where she needed to be.** Her global positioning and her international branding went to incredible heights because nothing replaced 'showing up'.

I activated this advice. In my industry, there was a major lack of representation from Indian influencers. I saw the gap in the market and I used my advantage of being located in Europe. I started attending international events. And the more I did, the more I got noticed and then invited to three more. So, ultimately, from just pretending that I had arrived, I did actually arrive. I didn't generate any revenue from this strategy for a while, but I was willing to invest in myself (in terms of time, energy and money) to build a greater brand.

I attended one presentation and one show out of the 50 that showcased, but I gained so much more. I understood how a fashion week works on the ground. It wasn't an unknown territory any more.

I learnt that even though I attended just one show, my audience loved all the content I created while I was at the fashion week. My engagement went up 40 per cent. I learnt that being out of my comfort zone pushed me to work harder. I needed to grab more of these uncomfortable situations.

By my second fashion week, later in 2018, I was a lot more prepared. For this run, I changed tack. I decided to first reach out to the Indian counterparts of the international brands showcasing there. In the fashion weeks of Paris and Milan, you're (usually) never paid to attend a show or an event. It's just good enough that you're invited! It's an investment for the person attending – i.e. me. So, instead of telling the brands that I would like to go for a fashion week and ask if they'd 'sponsor' me – my approach was, 'Hey, I am going for a fashion week to Paris and Milan. Are you hosting any events that I could cover on your behalf?'

I was personally investing in travel, lodging, expenses and accompanying team members but I knew I could make it fruitful.

I'll explain in brief: How did I make money and drive revenue for my business while attending a fashion week and upping my brand value? The revenue comes from supplemental brand collaborations. And what exactly is that? Well, a lot of brands are more than happy to do brand collaborations (paid ones) while you are travelling to these cities because this is the time when an influencer's reach and engagement is extremely high. It benefits the brand in question to feature on the influencer's page during this period. The approach would be to reach the fashion week a day prior or plan your calendar in a way that you have time to create content for these partnerships and then strategically drop the content online during the fashion week.

I got three positive responses for my second fashion week. I attended those events, networked, and got to know the global teams. It was Bvlgari that gave me my first opportunity. Over a dinner event, as I got to know the global Bvlgari team, they suddenly asked me if I was free (of course, I was – but I couldn't let that on right away!) the next morning to participate in a global campaign they were shooting with ten influencers from around the world with a famous photographer. It would be aired on all the global Bvlgari channels. They wanted me to be part of it. Me! My head exploded! This was huge and incredible.

And this is actually how I discovered the amazing GSD rule no. 7.

KEEP ROOM FOR THE UNEXPECTED

Leave some empty slots for magic to happen.

In life and in work (and in love), do things with a sense of hope and a sense of knowing that it could be bigger than what you could imagine. Keep space for pleasant surprises and bonuses. Give them breathing room to come alive.

Brand Masoom Minawala went from strength to strength every fashion week after 2018. Now, because I was working with a very small list of bigger global brands, I became a magnet for prominent Indian labels and also smaller indie designers. Working with Masoom meant their brand got featured alongside some big tickets, which in turn raised their brand value, recall and credibility in the market. For instance, at Cannes, while wearing jewellery from Bvlgari, I also wore Indian jewellery from a home-grown brand Karishma Joolry and my dad's Lion Jewellers. At a fashion week, while being dressed by Moncler and Hermes, I also wore a lot of Indian couture brands such as Amit Aggarwal and Gaurav Gupta, to name a few, along with some great but smaller labels like Anaash, my family's Cai Store, Chisel and Aprajita Toor.

Every time I went to a global event or attended a fashion week, the collaboration requests in my email exploded. The demand to be featured on my page would be up 60–70 per cent.

It started off with a simple GSD attitude. But, in 2022, international fashion weeks yielded the highest content engagement on my platform and the biggest spike in revenue ever. We were declining requests for shows because we had so many things on our calendar. We could only do a few key luxury houses in Milan and another seven-odd emerging ones.

Every time I go back to Paris or Milan, I go back to the same excitement and passion I felt at my first run in Paris – when I was enamoured just with the fact that I was there.

With fashion weeks ticked off my list by 2018, I was already dreaming about the other big key global fashion event, one of the largest in the world. The Festival De Cannes!

I wanted to go to the Cannes Film Festival – that much I knew. It was a vision in my head. It would add great value to my brand. And I eventually made it happen for myself in 2019.

Cannes Film Festival, 2019

While everyone and their aunties were gaping at the volume of Indian celebrities at Cannes in 2023, earlier on there were fewer invitees. It was a huge honour to be invited to the Cannes Film Festival and the red carpet run that comes with it. I first started researching on how I could get there via a simple Google search. I looked up all the smaller events that would take place at the festival and wrote to people (such as Chopard and Messika) saying I was going to be there and I'd love to attend their shows.

I got one invite.

I call this GSD rule no. 8.

IDENTIFY THE GOAL. THE PATH TO IT WILL REVEAL ITSELF

I was never really going to Cannes, but the GSD approach worked. 'You gotta start somewhere,' I told myself.

So I took a chance and reached out to the India team at L'Oréal and said I was going to Cannes and that I'd love to attend their event at the festival. 'Can we work something out?' I asked. My confident approach worked because they in turn felt confident enough to work with me. They took the idea to their global team, got approval, invited me to their event at Cannes and came back to me with a package. (A 'package' represents a comprehensive understanding of what is expected from both parties in the collaboration. It outlines the deliverables, commitments and compensation to ensure a mutually beneficial partnership.) And the idea came to life!

I now had two events to attend at Cannes. I landed in Cannes in 2019 with no dress, no idea what my experience would be, and no hint on whether there would even be a red carpet walk for me.

Bear in mind this is an event that celebrities spend six months on for their customized looks. I was scared and overwhelmed among vintage Chanel, Balmain couture and chic Cavalli, Halston, Dior and Jean Paul Gaultier. The biggest celebrities in the world were there with massive entourages. And here I was even doing my own make-up.

I felt so tiny, so irrelevant. I asked myself more than a dozen times what I was thinking by even wanting to be there. And, at the same time, I felt invincible. Representing India on the red carpet as a social media influencer, no matter how small that appearance, was a moment that overtook everything. I returned to Cannes two more times thereafter, building more relationships each time and gaining more confidence in my ability to represent myself on a global platform. I walked the red carpet at Cannes once in 2019 and twice in 2022 and three times in 2023.

THE GSD GUIDEBOOK

But how do you really get shit done? How do you even know where to start or what to do?

Here are my hacks:

1. **Jot down your dreams and goals on an Excel sheet** and check in on this every few months. Keep your goals well defined.

2. **Take a good look at what you've achieved and what challenges you have faced** in the past month/three months/year. Be super specific. Celebrate your victories and learn from your experience.

3. At every stage, make sure to **spell out exactly why you're doing what you're doing** and how it's going to make a positive difference to your goals.

My team and I meet every quarter, where we walk into a conference room with the attitude 'if there is a genie out there today who says yes to every goal of ours, what would we be asking for brand Masoom Minawala'? This includes BOTH short- and long-term goals. You can easily do this for yourself. In fact, you must. (I did it by myself, alone in a room for ten years straight.)

To illustrate this, here are some examples of what goes on our sheets:

Long-term goals

It might not happen immediately or in the coming quarters, but you **cannot lose sight of that goal.**

For me:
1. Being the face of a campaign (it finally happened in September 2022 when I became the face of Estée Lauder's Festive Campaign).
2. Being a part of the Forbes 30 under 30 list. This is something that has been on my list for years, and it happened in May 2022.

3. Publish my own book – it has been brewing in my mind for over four years now and it is finally happening.

4. Launch and grow a successful podcast – I genuinely think that the way I will be able to share content on a podcast would be very different from all the platforms I am currently on, but I am still figuring how to go about it, how I can create a difference and add value.

5. Launch a co-branded line with a beauty giant.

What are your long-term goals? It could be anything like (1) finish an online professional certificate course that will enhance my career and increase my potential salary; (2) earn ₹X lakh in three years; (3) chart my career change post five years; (4) investment plans.

Immediate goals

For these, it is essential to put up a timeline so that you know you need to make it happen or at least give it your best shot.

For me:

1. A one-year deal with a key player in each industry: technology, beauty, fashion.
2. An eight-figure deal.
3. Community growth of 30 per cent.
4. Do one CSR activity every time I am in India.
5. Impact small brands and fledgling entrepreneurs.

What about your short-term goals? Think about it. They could be to (1) finish a particular work project by a set date; (2) update my professional portfolio and CV; (3) attend at least one industry event to make contacts in a given quarter; (4) research on that promotion pitch or new business idea I have been procrastinating; (5) tackle the items on my to-do list that I have shelved for lack of time and/or interest.

FIVE

HOW TO NETWORK LIKE A BOSS

The ultimate guide for people who suck at small talk.

I have never been good at networking. It's not something I was born with. I'm not inherently a people's person and, frankly, I suck at small talk.

But networking is *critical* for success – whether you are a doctor, a lawyer or an influencer; whether you are an intern, a banker, an entrepreneur or at the CEO/CFO level. Networking is non-negotiable.

And why do I say that?

Well, I got invited to walk the red carpet at the Cannes Film Festival for a brand in my second year *while I was already at the festival* simply by speaking to a stranger in the elevator. I signed a seven-figure deal with a brand by reaching out to them on LinkedIn. Meeting a PR professional for coffee in Paris got me invited to the most prestigious and reputed charity gala in Europe.

To break it down very simply, networking tells you what the hell is going on in your industry. You find out what your peers are doing and how they're thinking and working. You get ideas for new ways of doing things. You get contacts to collaborate with. It amps up your professional confidence and profile and contributes to a sensible exchange of ideas and perspectives.

But I wasn't always comfortable with networking and putting myself out there. It was only during the period 2018–19 that I realized I had been a working girl for so long – six years plus – but I had built zero real professional relationships. I had just put blinders on and powered through my work. I hadn't spent time building a rapport with other professionals; so I had no mentors, no friendly peers, no one to share ideas with or grow with. In my case, my target crowd would consist of PR people or brand reps, but broadly speaking networking expands to peers, colleagues, people in the same industry as you.

Perhaps if I had 'networked' back then, I would have been much further along in my career today.

BUT I JUST DIDN'T FEEL LIKEABLE

You see, my biggest weakness at the beginning of my career – and for several years thereafter, to be honest – was that I just didn't think I was likeable. Why? There may be a few reasons but a big one was the fact that at the beginning of my blogging years, my work was most often acknowledged negatively – as a joke; something to be made fun of, laughed at, criticized.

Let me go back to an incident that occurred long ago involving an old friend. It was at the beginning of my content-creation journey. This friend would imitate how I posed or spoke in my posts and stories for a laugh at gatherings. Recalling now, it does sound super silly. But when you're in your early 20s and you hear you're being made fun of in a group, it kinda kills your self-esteem. There were multiple incidents like these. Acquaintances would tell my friends, my friends would tell me. In fact, some of my own friends would make unkind comments and that would reach me too. I was suddenly an easy 'topic of discussion' because my work was public. Of course, I tried my hand at figuring out why this was happening, by sharing how I felt with them. But it was draining. If my friends weren't taking me seriously – would others?

As I have already shared elsewhere in this book too, barely a handful of people were supportive and motivating through my early career years. Most others thought I was screwing around or simply doing something that seemed useless and childish. Side note: **It may be**

the people closest to you or just outside your innermost circle who will find a change in direction and motivation in you the hardest to swallow and cheer. Basically, they think they know you. Many people I knew couldn't get with the programme: the Masoom who spent her college days eating chowmein in a canteen was now a driven, motivated, serious content-creator-businesswoman. They just didn't get it.

How could I muster up the confidence to 'network' when this is what people I knew thought of me? How could I go to the brand manager of a major company and tell them that I was a value proposition for reaching new audiences if most people around me felt I was a joke? The general atmosphere had damaged my self-confidence.

At the same time, even though I would mostly stay in my shell, most people who didn't even know me thought the opposite about me: That I networked like a crazy leech. I would pull favours like no one's business. That my success was because of the privilege of inherited contacts. Talk about being an equal-opportunity punching bag!

This is a massive misconception about me. I have had no networks and contacts that opened doors for me through my family or friends. I wasn't in any position to 'use networks' as I had none.

When PR companies and brands started hosting India's initial events for bloggers, I attended a couple. By the fourth one, I came to say, 'I don't do events' and 'I'm happy to support your brand in any way I can; I'll even post about the event if you send me pictures. But I just can't manage coming to events while running two businesses.'

Absolute lie.

I wasn't so busy that I couldn't make time. I was just so uncomfortable at the first three events I attended that I didn't have the courage to go for any more. I vividly remember being at one of Estée Lauder's events (they were disruptive in accepting the creator industry from the get-go) and I had felt so lost. I did not know how to strike up a conversation with anyone. I had spent so much time getting ready for it and I left with no photographs because I was too awkward to ask someone to take them for me. I just stood in a corner and watched people schmooze around me.

And even if I could bring myself to talk to people with the aim of networking, I worried constantly about rejection. I once went for a magazine shoot that was featuring disruptors in the fashion industry. I went with the conscious intention of being friendly. There was a stylist on the set I got along great with and we even managed to have a warm conversation. Two days later, I tried making small talk with her over social media and I got no response. Ghosted. Now you see – I had pushed myself out of my comfort zone to strike up a conversation and make that effort. And what was the feeling I was left with? 'Clearly, I wasn't good enough for her to want to reply to me.'

Around 2018, like any given Sunday, I was doing some mild competitor analysis against another influencer who I completely envied (more on that later in Chapter 7). No harm in crossing your Ts and dotting your Is, right? I kept noticing her at various events. Every time she made these appearances, she would always take photos with the PR person, marketing head and brand head. I thought, 'Am I missing something here?' She would somehow get the best breaks. Why was she able to get these special and elevated opportunities as compared to me and other influencers of the same calibre?

The answer: she had built strong professional relationships – not only with the most powerful or glamorous person in the room but also with the people who ran the show on the ground.

That was the tipping moment for me. That's when I

decided I had to overcome this personal challenge, or mental block if you will. I had to do it for my career. **As a go-getter in any stage of your working life, you just have to get comfortable talking to people, being more brazen, introducing yourself and building connections.** It took a lot of effort from me, but I had witnessed it working well for someone else right there in front of me. And I had to take inspiration from her. Learning by watching.

When I finally did step out of my comfort zone and start building professional relationships, it was so awkward. Okay, it was hella awkward at first but once I became good at it, I started to like it. None of this was an organic process for me, by the way. At first, I had to force myself to do it. I thought of it as pure business development. **Networking was a chore, something I just had to get done with. Like you take your vitamins or do your taxes.** However, I built great professional relationships only when I gained confidence in myself. And I had to work on that self-confidence.

How did I work on my self-confidence? I had to repeatedly tell myself I was good enough. We all have SOMETHING going for us. I was successful. I had thousands of people coming in daily to see what I had to say. I ignored all the other BS and focused on just this piece of information. **So if you have something (ANYTHING) going for you, just put blinders on and ignore all the ifs and buts and what-ifs and focus on that.** I also did this using my favourite tool: Affirmations.

1. I'm a creative genius.
2. I am strong, confident and brilliant.
3. I know how to build connections with like-minded people.
4. I trust my intuition.
5. I am proud of my accomplishments, big and small.
6. Networking helps me take my business to the next level.

It's only human to take personal rejections very harshly. It's human to feel unlikeable. You'd be surprised at how many of us are in the same boat. But the bottom line is this: **You cannot let anyone else's response to you or their perception of you determine your self-worth. There will be people who don't respond to you, places where you don't click. And equally, there will be people with whom you get on like a house on fire. You'll never discover the good connections unless you are brave enough to deal with the failed connections.** It's a part of life!

RULE 1: START SLOW. AND LET IT COME FROM A PLACE OF AUTHENTICITY

Once I had worked on my self-confidence and affirmations, I started my journey with networking or building professional relations very slowly. It would first be someone I truly wanted to connect with, a brand I really wanted to work with or someone I genuinely admired. I simply reached out and connected via cold phone calls or cold DMs. It was also easier for me to meet in quiet settings one-on-one than at loud noisy events with a hundred people bustling around the place.

I soon also figured it's best to be yourself. Don't try to game the situation. Don't try to say the things you feel the other person needs to hear if they are to like you. It's not a sustainable choice. Only when you are your true authentic self will you be able to present yourself as a true fit – for friendship or work collabs. People always know – maybe consciously, maybe unconsciously — if you are being authentic or just fakin' it to 'get something' from them. I had to come from a place of honesty and authenticity if I wanted to do this the right way. Just be yourself.

RULE 2: TAKE THAT FIRST STEP AND JUST START CONNECTING

Over five years ago I had signed up for an entrepreneurship course online. It was a target task for my course to make a list of people I wished to connect with and then reach out to all those people.

I sat down and made a list of people I would like to network with: global influencers, brand representatives, leading designers and very senior PR people – those who at the time I felt were 'out of my reach, but I would love to connect with'. I might have worked with some of their team members down the hierarchy, but I didn't have a personal connection with anyone from my list.

I decided I would reach out to my list, no matter what the response. Well, as part of my coursework, I had to do the 'reaching out' or risk getting an F.

Instagram was the best way to get this rolling. I was so nervous. After much ado, I finally drafted a casual message telling these people that I'd like to connect. What if they thought I was a freak? What if they sent screenshots of my message on WhatsApp groups? Hitting the send button was hard for me and I had to really force myself to do it. But I was shocked at the number of responses I got. My message to them had no demands and no agenda

– I just wanted to connect in general. **People find it very hard to say no to someone who has requested them to spare time for a phone call of just five to ten minutes or a short coffee meeting.** It was a game-changer for me. I always thought so many people were out of my reach, but one message received so many positive responses – so the block was really in my mind. From this point onwards, things got easier. I had gained the confidence to JUST REACH OUT. I wasn't afraid any more.

MAKE A NETWORKING BUCKET LIST

I would highly recommend this exercise. Open Word, StickyNote, OneNote, Monday.com, ClickUp – whatever you want. Use plain old paper otherwise. Make two lists of people you'd like to network with (1) those around you, within your possible reach (with some effort), set with a timeline, and (2) your 'out-of-my-reach' dream list, with no timeline.

Whenever you have some spare time, add notes alongside each name from lists 1 and 2 on how it may be possible to connect with them, like upcoming professional events where you may be able to meet them, people whom you may have in common and so on. Send them LinkedIn messages or a DM or an email or a WhatsApp. Whatever. Just do it. And don't forget about this list. Keep revisiting it, editing it, adding to it and, yes, crossing people off from it!

RULE 3: IT'S NOT A TRANSACTION

Not everyone will always welcome you with open arms, and that's fine. The biggest red flag that people watch out for, and can be a huge turn-off, is transactional language. 'Do this for me, and I will do that for you.' Avoid this at all costs.

My life coach (who I started working with in June 2021) taught me this about building professional relationships. And it was a valuable lesson indeed. Let me share it here. **Whenever you meet someone new or form a new relationship, never speak of what you want from them. Ask instead, 'How can I help you?', 'What can I do for you?'** I loved this approach! Networking is not as selfish as perceived. I wouldn't advise people to network to gain something. It's a two-way street. It's a collaboration. You are also bringing something to the table, and that's a more interesting way of looking at it.

RULE 4: DON'T THINK OF IT AS A PROFESSIONAL 'HOOK-UP'. IT'S A RELATIONSHIP.

One of my most meaningful working relationships has been with one of the world's largest luxury houses that has a prominent base in India. Their global team knows me as I represent them from India on a global platform, one of the only Indian candidates to attend international events on their behalf. And I cracked this whole relationship with one random Instagram DM in 2018.

It was a cold connect with the PR and Communications manager of the brand who is now a very close friend. I just wrote: 'Hi, it's good to connect with you. I am in Mumbai and it would be great to catch up over a cup of coffee.' She wrote back and we met. I was so nervous. This was a huge meeting and I prepped for hours about what I would say. I showed up at the five-star hotel coffee shop she had invited me to and I was met with not just her but two of her colleagues as well. Apparently, she had limited time and I overlapped on her meeting with others. I took a seat. For the first 30 minutes, it seemed like they were having their own meeting and I was eavesdropping. You know when others are having a conversation you know nothing about and you feel like an intruder? Yes, that.

Later, she turned to me and asked a few questions

about myself and my work. Very quickly she went on to tell me how her luxury house had no digital presence yet and did not think they would be doing any sort of associations with creators and influencers in the near future. It was simply not part of their media plan. Their focus was advertising in luxury magazines. Any prospect of us doing anything together was closed even before it started. I was so disappointed. I thought I had a foot in the door with that meeting. We wrapped up almost immediately and headed towards the exit.

While walking out, she spontaneously invited me to tag along for an event she had to attend. I said yes, sure, why not. (After a quick reminder to myself that this was NOT about what she could bring to the table – it was not meant to be transactional, right?). In the car ride and at the event, what happened was this: I built a personal rapport with her. I didn't want anything from her and she had not much to gain from me but what we really bonded over was working in the luxury industry and being young women trying to find our way in the world. It was light, fun and from a place of friendship without demands or expectations. We stayed in touch.

Fast forward one year. Suddenly, one day, the same luxury house's entire marketing strategy had changed.

They wanted to focus on digital marketing, led by influencers. And who was the first person on her radar? Obviously, me.

I cannot network 'for the sake of it'. And it's probably like that for many others like me. **What I prefer is to be able to build and nurture real relationships involving people I can have real connections with. If they can benefit me professionally, that's a plus but not a pre-condition.** I believe it is okay to protect your energy by chasing real relationships and not transactional ones. It is okay to avoid overexposing yourself and having relationships with every person you meet.

My approach is more 'micro networking'; niche and specified. I would much rather be selective about the people I give access to my energy and whose energy I can access. You can get very far in life with a few deep connections that hold value. I prefer that I reach out to and respond to people's energies rather than their profiles. That's been my mantra when it comes to networking.

If I had to explain it in one line, I'd say real networking is not a professional 'hook-up'; it's a relationship.

HOW TO TALK TO STRANGERS

1. One of my favourite tricks from my husband when it comes to people (he is the most loved person in any room) is this. People love talking. Especially about themselves. Just ask the questions. And be genuinely interested in their answers. Once they answer, ask follow-up questions. The ice will just vanish.

2. I once read in a book: always have a strong opinion. Don't be vanilla. Take a stand, don't sit on the fence. People will remember you more for disagreeing with them (politely, in a friendly manner) than if you just nod along like a wallflower.

3. Show up with honesty. I am always asked so many questions about my job. Everyone is so curious about how this works. And instead of giving them the politically correct fluff they expect to hear, I tell it like it is. The good, the bad, the ugly. I say it's tough. I say it's frustrating at times to show up online every day. And that honesty – that's relatable. Also, throw in a useful tip or two. People respond really well to that.

SIX

A 12-YEAR RECIPE

. . . of creating, adapting and reinventing, and experiencing the magic.

Let me jump right into it.

I learnt one pretty valuable life lesson in my professional journey quite early on.

The secret to success is the ability to ride out a stormy wave – whether it is because of an error you made or a bad surprise that was thrown at you. There are always failures, mistakes, setbacks, misses, changes and bad days. But you obviously don't stop. You adapt, learn and course correct. You ride it out. You reinvent yourself. You move to Version 2.0. And then to 3.0 and beyond.

As I've mentioned earlier in this book too, my life coach always tells me, 'It doesn't matter how hard or how many times you fall. It matters how fast you get up.'

And to adapt a Western saying to India: **when life gives you lemons, you make achaar.**

Of course, I also do take some time off to sulk. Whining is good. I let it out. A bad day often only gets worse by the end of it. So, when something really bad happens, I often just end the day right there and then. And maybe take a nap. A good nap does wonders.

WHEN THINGS CHANGE, YOU CHANGE

Not all change feels cataclysmic like the Covid-19 pandemic (more on that in a bit). **Some change just quietly seeps into everyday life. But, before you know it, that change has altered the game completely. So you still have to be on top of it.**

When I first started, I poured my heart into and spent multiple nights on my blog, where written content was the main focus. It allowed me to express myself and build a community. My blog gave me a platform to connect with my audience authentically. But things were changing rapidly. As new platforms emerged, I quickly understood the importance of visuals in storytelling. I embraced the shift to visual-first platforms, integrating stunning images into my content. It resonated like never before with my followers. As the landscape evolved further, video became the new frontier.

Embracing this change felt challenging at first. Throughout my journey, I encountered various platforms that came and went, like Facebook, Clubhouse and Tiktok.

A lot of people told me to not hop on to these bandwagons – they thought some platforms weren't a right fit for my brand. But I tried them, and my community loved having me there. I embraced each opportunity as it presented itself to me. Being an early adapter played a crucial role in my growth. I've never been one to shy away from trying something new. **Staying adaptable is key to thriving in any dynamic workplace.**

There's a lesson here for everyone going forward, for almost every profession. In some way or another, you have to stay on top of tech trends no matter what. This is no longer a question of just seeming cool and relevant or just for social networking or entertainment. It is increasingly a matter of survival. My team, for instance, has started experimenting with AI tools to keep on top of things . . . It's going to be increasingly hard to dodge the change that's coming.

But other kinds of change were also so big bang! In 2020, Covid and the global lockdown changed the way half the world operated and most aspects and elements of my business dropped – shows, events, fashion weeks, paid collaborations; dressing up, shooting, the glitz and the glam. So I went back to how I had started. Creating content for the joy of creating – just a phone on a tripod, an audience and my thoughts, opinions, perspectives and what was already in my wardrobe. I was shooting DAILY for HOURS. I was LOVING IT. I had fully come into my own and I felt like I was able to communicate this through my content. Funny thing – my audience was able to see that. I was having fun with my content with transitions, throwing dresses, doing multiple outfit changes, implementing crazy, offbeat edits – and they devoured it.

There were several content creators and influencers across the world who just stopped creating content during the pandemic. That's so understandable. Many people's mental health was in a fragile place. Plus 'cancel culture' was peaking and people were scared of taking the wrong step. Some creators simply did not enjoy the process of creating within the four walls of their homes. The industry in many ways was falling apart. Creators who had started with me stopped posting altogether. This was also the time I received buckets of unreasonable online hate with a mix of valid criticism for some of my content pieces. There was a palpable shift in the industry and I was scared that if I didn't tread carefully, I too would lose my job and get 'cancelled' for good one day.

Being able to understand that your work is in danger – having that awareness – this is a #redalert moment. And taking action at the right time is important. If you

are not aware and are unable to course correct, you're at risk. Slowly but surely, you will see the signs of danger: the cracks, the change in mood, the warnings. Act fast.

CHANGE IS THE ONLY CONSTANT

During the pandemic, I knew the mood of my audience was changing. (Mine had changed too; I lost two family members in the span of a few months.) They expected more awareness and sensitivity from me. And I am glad that they did. I reshuffled my perspectives too. At a time when the world was going through a crisis that had upended lives and families, relationships and livelihoods, I took a step back to think about how I could add value to people around me. Could I tap my network? I actively started helping people with detailed resources on oxygen cylinders and hospital beds. I raised over ₹50 lakh in 24 hours for a fund started with the Hemkunt Foundation for oxygen cylinders.

I also realized that a lot of Indian home-grown brands, designers and artisans were having a tough run of things and were on the brink of shutting down. And so I launched a not-for-profit initiative called 'Support Indian Designers', where I promoted these aforementioned labels on my platform, leveraging my community, for no cost to them. Brands got visibility and the audience got access to new information. It was my way of giving back to the industry that had quite honestly given me the joy of a job I loved so much. **(P.S.: I learnt that you must never forget where you came from and what makes you stand where you do.)** It was a ROARING success and it continues to be one of my most impactful endeavours. The hashtag #SupportIndianDesigners has over 7,27,000 posts to date and has had a dramatic impact on so many of the small businesses we supported during the pandemic. The brands that I showcased reported huge jumps in their followers and actual, tangible SALES.

One brand reported such a surge of orders for the outfit I posted that their karigars nicknamed it the 'Masoom joda'.

Another brand sold out their featured outfit within days.

A home-grown saree brand said they were on the brink of shutting down because of the pandemic but my post helped them resurface.

An entrepreneur wrote in telling me she got multiple orders from Australia and the US through my post.

It's important to note that during the pandemic, views and engagement were at an all-time high. The internet was

Love from under #SupportIndianDesigners

Mentioned you in their story

Add to your story

We are on our 69th order that came because of you. Made a separate list of the "masoom magic" orders!
The sales has gone up INSANELY!
Thank you is an understatement 🙏
Thank you for blessing our small business. Will never forget this.

Lots of love from us 🫂

Double-tap to 🖤

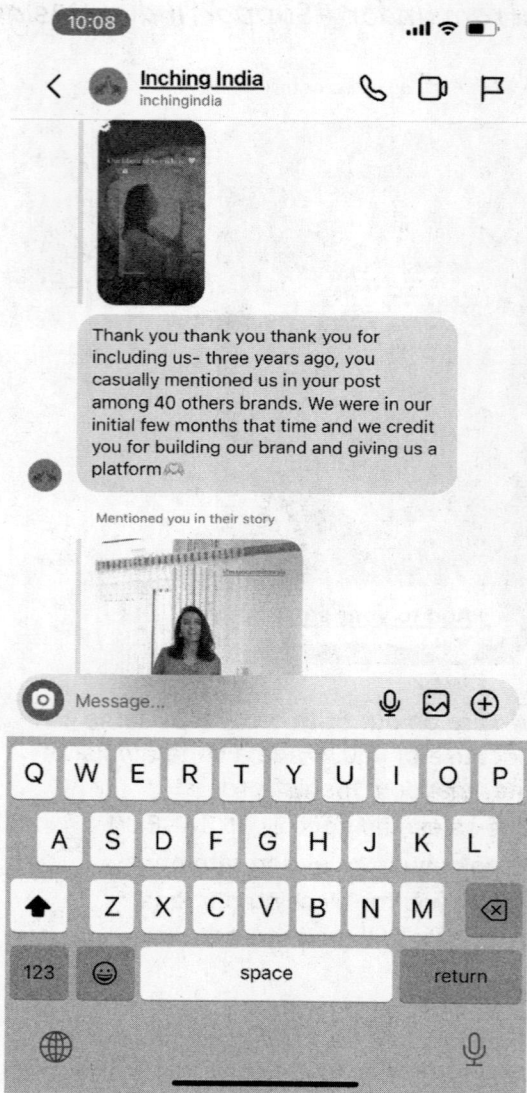

Thank you thank you thank you for including us- three years ago, you casually mentioned us in your post among 40 others brands. We were in our initial few months that time and we credit you for building our brand and giving us a platform 🫶

Mentioned you in their story

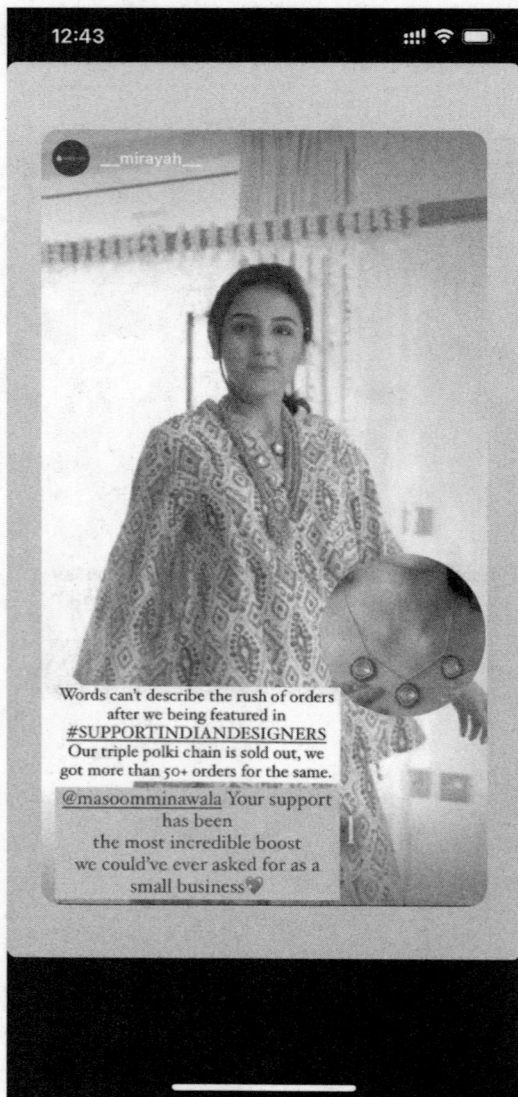

12:43

__mirayah__

Words can't describe the rush of orders after we being featured in #SUPPORTINDIANDESIGNERS Our triple polki chain is sold out, we got more than 50+ orders for the same.

@masoomminawala Your support has been the most incredible boost we could've ever asked for as a small business🖤

10:20   .il 4G 🔋

< (Dc) **Label DC**   📞 📹 🚩
       dcmumbai

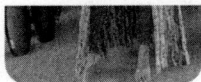

19:55

Ms Minawala, we have been long time admirers of your work and have tried to mirror the same ethics in our own line of business. You have no idea how many people you inspire each day. To go through the trouble to shoot 100 pieces, sort them, iron them, co-ordinate with designers, receive a 1000 packages - all pro bono - who does that in today's age? Thank you for doing this for @dcmumbai. We'll make sure we pay this forward. You changed our fate today and for that, we'll be indebted to you for life. :)

Mentioned you in their story

Add to your story

💬 Message...   🎤 🖼️ ⊕

1:01   .ıll 4G 🔋

threethree.store
Business chat

You mentioned @threethree.store in your story

Mentioned you in their story

Mentioned you in their story

28 OCT 2021

Replied to your story

You make our lehenga look beautiful Masoom! 🖤 ◎

27 AUG 2022

Mentioned you in their story

11:01

Hi Masoom!
Your haul video got us all pumped up with the amazing response! 🚀

It's been three days since you posted and we are still receiving orders and dms on what we now famously call the 'Masoom Set' 🎉

We love how you look out for brands and your audience together.

Thanks a bunch!

Love,
Team
Three|Three

Message...

being consumed like it had never been consumed before. Everyone was home and glued to their screens and what were they watching? Content creators.

And I kept churning content series after series, IP after IP, trend after trend, sometimes even three posts a day, to capitalize on the heightened views. One such IP called #IndiaILove was picked up by Instagram India in 2022 and made into a national IP on the occasion of Independence Day. So when the industry finally rolled back into business post lockdown, I had tripled my following, now standing at a million-plus followers and I was charging four times more than before the pandemic.

And so it was that at the peak of the pandemic, I was hiring new people. I decided to procure a specific content consultant, a so far non-existent department in my team. I had been solely handling all aspects of planning, ideating and executing content all this while. However, with the introduction of a content consultant, the workload was effectively shared along with an infusion of fresh perspectives and expertise. This allowed me to focus on other critical and creative tasks. In six months, my team had doubled. I had an intern based out of the US, a video editor, a data analyst and my content consultant turned full time. This was a game-changer for me and led to a huge shift in my way of thinking.

This brings me to the final section – on riding out those stormy waves, making that achaar and proving that you have to keep updating, adapting and recalibrating your life and your work to move on. To succeed.

'MASOOM MAGIC': 12 YEARS IN THE MAKING

I am willing to change – year after year. And that has always opened doors for me.

While growing up an Average Jane, did I ever, ever imagine that I'd evolve from a blogger taking photos in her building compound to a digital entrepreneur with a catchphrase coined just for her?

Today, there is this catchphrase that goes around. And the best part? It's been coined by my community, not by me. It's called 'Masoom Magic'. And what is this 'Masoom Magic' you ask? Brands claim it's the 'magic' that touches them whenever I post about them leading to awareness, eyeballs, followers, sales and more.

I'm humbled to say that brands have sold out their entire collection in a week with my endorsement. There have been multiple scenarios where websites have crashed with the traffic after my post went viral. At times, I have recommended some changes to an outfit that I feel would work better. And the brands have actually

Masoom Magic

noticed the impact when their customers chose to go with my exact outfit. Since my followers are based globally, brands have had sales from around the world with my recommendation. Pieces that are worn by me are often bestsellers for months. A start-up clothing brand tried different forms of promotions, which got some visibility. But one post by me and their followers increased by 700 per cent overnight and generated their first-ever sales. For several months later, they continued to get more followers through my old post with enquiries about the outfit I had worn.

On an Instagram story that lasted 24 hours, a brand received about 250 orders for pieces in the range of ₹3,000 approximately from my unique link. Another vendor got more than 247 orders in five days for an outfit priced at ₹9,000 and is still one of their bestsellers. An Indian wear label got over 150 orders for a pre-draped saree priced at ₹30,000 and over 120 orders for a lehenga priced at ₹50,000 that I posted about. A prominent Indian designer brand sold more than 60 lehengas priced at approximately ₹170,000 each in a few days.

I am not just a girl taking photos any more because I am now a girl giving you an ROI (return on investment) better than any other marketing channel.

Everyone asks me – what's the secret behind this

'Masoom Magic'? I can never find the words to explain to them that the Masoom Magic has been 12 years in the making. And 12 years of simply recalibrating when I needed to. I have tried every permutation-computation under the sun to perfect my formula and somehow along the way I got so lucky that I was able to build the most incredible community of like-minded women on the internet. And these like-minded women have given me the most precious thing anyone in the world ever could – TRUST. And this trust is the very foundation of what the world sees as brand Masoom Minawala.

But you see, there was a deeper impact at a human level on me as a person. What this trust also gave me was a sense of belief in myself. I don't know whether it was that I finally started having fun with my content, embraced my honest self on the internet, found my purpose in supporting a community of entrepreneurs or just the sheer fact that there had been so many ups and downs already, I wasn't scared of the wave any more. Ten years into the journey, I began to bloom. I was fulfilled, I felt unbreakable and I reflected that. I didn't care about hearing a 'No' any more because I knew it would never pierce my armour. In fact it was okay if there was a 'No' – it would be their loss. I didn't care about falling down so much, because I knew I would get up, I had done it already. I found that accepting yourself and finding success on the inside also translated into success on the outside. My inner acceptance of what my journey had been and my resilience to keep going was finally visible to others and the 'Yeses began to pour in. Before I knew it, I was a showstopper for a show at Milan Fashion Week, an event which I had aggressively struggled to just get a seat at. Front-lining it was a far-fetched dream. Attending Louis Vuitton shows front row in Paris and Seoul. Being on multiple covers, digital and/or print, of magazines including *Elle*, *Entrepreneur* and *Travel & Leisure*. Being on the *GQ* 30 Most Influential Young Indians list. Winning the 'Most Authentic Fashion Influencer' Award at Cannes. Winning the 'Luxury Fashion Influencer of the Year' three years in a row from *Cosmopolitan*. In fact there was one week where I had three major wins and I felt overwhelmed by the joy of it. I walked the runway for Abu Jani Sandeep Khosla and it felt like life had come full circle since they were the first Indian designers to put their faith in me during my virtual wedding. I was the showstopper at an India Fashion Week show when I was seven months pregnant, and that moment is still etched in my mind for how powerful it felt to walk down the runway with my new body and still have it celebrated. I am so very grateful for these experiences.

THE BUSINESS OF INFLUENCING

It's not just craft or creativity or hard work or fluttering around an editing app. There is a solid, rapidly evolving and very dynamic business that has kept this influencing industry alive for the past decade and booming for the past five.

- It's about perfecting your product. In my industry, the product is CONTENT.

- It's about building a community. Understanding who your audience is, where they come from, what their likes and dislikes are and bringing them together to form a rock-solid coterie.

- It's about consistency. My community trusts me because I have been showing up consistently for 12 years. 12 YEARS. And not a day missed. I am a lot more dependable than most of their friends.

- It's about identifying your USP. I found mine in being the most honest version of myself on the internet. My community loves my authenticity, my relatability, my honesty.

- It's about relationships, like the one you have with your community or the one you have with your partners (the brands: pro bono, paid, the ones giving you stuff for sourcing – every single one) and the one you have with yourself because it's a piece of you that you give away every day through your product.

SEVEN

WHY YOU GOTTA LOVE COMPETITION

A little rivalry, of the right kind.

From a purely theoretical point of view, your competitor is a peer, someone doing the work you want to do.

In my head, it's someone like Deepika Padukone.

But is *she* my competition?

Obviously not.

She is far more successful and established than I am. She is a global ambassador for large luxury brands, which is something I would absolutely love to do in this life. That is my goal. In my head, I would like to 'compete' with Deepika. It's how you take things a notch higher for yourself.

THE LEARNER LICENCE

Look, I get that it sounds a bit (a lot?) delulu that I think of Deepika when I think of my competition. Maybe what

I'm trying to say is that **rather than overthinking about competition with my peers to goad myself to do better, I prefer to focus on role models. Role models don't come with the same edge as 'competing' with your peers.** Light-bulb moment!

I have a vivid memory from my past where I had felt very threatened by another influencer. The kind of focus I gave it had a very negative twist on my life. It made me feel low about myself and my work. I had noticed this influencer at every event, getting fabulous opportunities that other influencers and I were never privy to. (She's the person I mentioned in Chapter 5, the one who always had access to the best opportunities because she networked like a queen.) Feeling 'threatened' was a very demeaning emotion. And, honestly, I didn't like the way I behaved as a result. In conversations with others and with myself, I would always be picking on her flaws to make myself feel better, like 'Oh, she's bought the followers', 'What has she done to her face' or 'Everything about her is gimmicky'.

I bet you do this too. When a peer is doing well, lots of us may tend to tell ourselves a story that connects the dots of their success to a cause other than them and their hard work. Or we tell ourselves a story of how they aren't successful at all, how the success is a sham, a show, etc. I get that. **Sometimes it's hard to digest the success of a peer. I was like that too. But for God's sake, let's all stop doing that. It's petty, small-minded and just a plain waste of time.**

That's where Deepika comes in – or Priyanka Chopra, whom I mentioned in Chapter 4. Why do you think biographies are such a successful genre of non-fiction? Why do many top CEOs of the world's best companies love reading biographies? Because by focusing your attention on and studying the best minds of this world or of your industry, you are getting life lessons from the very best. You can study their lives, their strategies, their career trajectories, their weaknesses, their strengths . . . **Rather than only or always focusing on your colleagues, focus on your seniors or super-seniors – like the boss's boss's boss.** That's the way to be better every day. Observe them, learn from their journeys. Talk and question. There's so much to absorb.

But coming back to competition with peers and feeling the need to trash-talk the ones who are doing well – one day, a switch flipped in my head, and I thought, rather than spending my time bitching, what can I learn from them? Look, I know this sounds super preachy and goody-goody but the honest truth is this: **I can either spend my**

time being bitchy or I can just, well, move on and learn from my competition. It not only saves my mental sanity but is also a great way to get ahead.

Since my mindset change, the work of my peers has been a great learning curve for me. It can be the same for you. In fact, competition has led me to question my decisions. It's led me to look at my work and frown and know that I could have done better. It's made me more determined.

While I don't keep an eye on what my peers are doing all the time, I do some moderate stalking every so often. When I first started blogging at 19, I didn't do any 'competition analysis'. To be honest, there was no one to analyse locally. The only blogger at the time was Amitabh Bachchan who promoted his blog on his Twitter handle and there was no way I could compete with him! But as I moved into creating content more seriously and 'full time', I did a deep dive across the board. I began to study and track what my peers were doing across the world.

I analysed a few things like their product, their content offering and also their target audience, their marketing strategies and their overall positioning in the market. This helped me understand what I needed to do in order to differentiate (and better) myself from them so that I could position myself as a better alternative and gain a competitive advantage.

There have been so many times when I was inspired by what others were doing; so many things that I could adapt in my work. The outcome or result would always be lukewarm or terrible. Later, I decided to carve my unique path in content creation – i.e. not blindly copy trends that other content creators and influencers are setting. That's when the result was always phenomenal. **If you're too busy following a benchmark set by someone else so to speak, you won't have the time or bandwidth to be the one that stands out.**

What I mean is that you don't always need to 'be inspired' by your peers or your competition. I do, however, think **it is very interesting to examine other people's work.** Look at what they're doing right and what they're doing wrong. Observe, track and identify strengths and weaknesses. **Are they applying any practices or strategies that you could apply, but you've missed out on so far? How can you make the same impact and progress as them?**

In my book, this is by far a more constructive and proactive approach to competition.

Competition has acted as motivation for me: to 'keep up', to be better, to continue adapting. The fear that if I don't continue to adapt I will be left behind has been quite a driving force for me.

On that note, let me add that **while it's important to stay aware of your 'competition' and learn from them, it's equally important to be strategic about who you consider to be your competition. I don't hand over that 'competitor' title freely.** Be selective about who you track, who you give your mindspace to.

ARE YOU DOING BETTER THAN YOU DID YESTERDAY?

Babies lift their heads before they start to roll over. Then they learn to sit unaided before they can stand. They surf a room, holding on to furniture before they can walk on their own. You benchmark your baby's progress based on what they were able to do yesterday. You don't wonder why they aren't running marathons when they are still at the crawling stage!

The most important thing is to see if you're doing better today than yesterday, last week, last month, last quarter, last year . . . What I want to do is compete with myself. Everyone follows a different pace and has a different place. It doesn't help to constantly benchmark yourself against others. **Benchmark against yourself.** This is critical.

It is so damn easy to get carried away by what others are doing and thinking 'Why am I not here, not doing this thing, not attending that party, not in the photo?' But no one else is you. **You are in your own lane. Be consistent and run at your own speed.**

MORE 'COMPETITION' EQUALS MORE GROWTH

I am a huge believer in abundance. **At my core, I feel there is truly enough for everyone.** We live in a country and era of opportunity. Let me use my industry as an example. India has a deep and voluminous content creator industry. Every time there's been a surge of new entrants in my space – and I've been lucky enough to see that surge more than four times in the last decade – I've taken it as a resounding confirmation that my industry is about to go places. And I'm going to be right here, in this seat, leading it. I think of it as a fraternity. If everyone does well, I do well.

If Influencer X breaks a glass ceiling by being the first creator to get the honour of being a showstopper for a big-ticket fashion show, then the concept has been proven and next season, I could get the same opportunity. If Influencer Y becomes the face of a major brand, then guess what? My chances of becoming the face of another major brand have just gone up. In any young industry, you have to realize you're in this together. We're building the industry together, not just competing with each other.

From this thought stemmed Schbang MMaximize, an influencer management agency I co-founded in 2022, designed to handle 'influencing' strategies for celebrities, designers, creators, anyone.

But for the first year, I struggled to sign on talent. Everyone thought 'Why sign up with Masoom's agency? She will keep all the plum work for herself.' People wondered why I was setting up a company that would 'help' my own competition and give them the information I had so painstakingly gathered.

My career was one heck of a difficult journey for me to crack. I was trying to make international fashion weeks and the Cannes Film Festival happen for myself when almost nobody in my space was doing it. I was one of the first Indian influencers to make my way in. At international fashion weeks, I probably did four years of 2–3 seasons a year, so it was a minimum of 12 seasons of work after which we saw a massive influx of Indian influencers. This was after I had done detailed videos of my insights into how international fashion week events work, how to get invited, what happens there, what happens at a show, how you get into a show, how to network, and so on. I did it because I love my job, it is part of my work and it was a new way for me to create interesting content for my community and share solid information. Also, guess what, **if your secret sauce is 'gatekeeping' or withholding information, then you're missing a trick.** It won't take anyone too far in life. **Especially not in an internet age where information spreads like wildfire.**

In my book, if people are watching my content and becoming creators or becoming better creators than me, it does not mean I am generating more competition for myself. It means I am adding to the growth of my industry. I cannot single-handedly take the industry anywhere, right? I need other players. This is my mantra.

If I am setting up an agency to help other influencers, for instance, I know that I have been able to crack some codes in this space that I would love to help others crack in order to take their business to the next level. It aligns with my passion and my purpose.

I live a life that is professionally fulfilling. I really want other people to get professional satisfaction from a job they love. That's why I am passionate about this agency. There's a reason why my team often calls me 'irritatingly optimistic'. I guess I am guilty of that. But never forget, a rising tide lifts all boats . . .

EIGHT

MASOOM MINUS INSTAGRAM

Who am I when there is no work?

As an influencer, social media is in my blood and bones. My profession demands I am always on and hyperconnected. I guess that's true for a lot of us, even if we aren't 'influencers'.

But that isn't the entirety of my life – thank God! There is a significant Masoom beyond the internet.

I am a woman most often seen in a pair of pyjamas at home, hair up in a semi-messy bun (and I don't mean salon-level thoughtfully dishevelled). You're most likely to catch me with no make-up and bare feet, loving my glass of chaas and a bowl of tamatar nu shaak. And like most self-respecting Gujaratis, I get cranky when I am hungry. This is also a way for me to say: guys, **what you see on the internet isn't fully real. That's not the aggregate of a person's life.** No matter how glossy it looks, the brutal truth is we are all more similar than we sometimes realize.

Working from home right after the comfort of a home-cooked lunch is the most favourite part of my job. I work best when I am alone in my bedroom; just me, my laptop, phone and diary. And I do work very hard.

I think my most striking feature is that I am self-aware. I know I am not the prettiest girl in the room, but I am the most hard-working one. And, in any situation, I am very trusting that what's meant to be mine will come my way.

MY REGIMEN OR THE LACK THEREOF

Contrary to what people may believe – given this very public Instagram life of mine – I have no strict or complicated food, fitness or beauty routine.

The one routine that I have been dedicated to is my practice of gratitude. The first thing I do in the morning when I wake up is walk to the bathroom, and for every step I take from the moment my feet hit the ground, I say 'Thank You'. I read this in a book years ago and it has stuck with me for the last seven years of my life. So, before I begin my day, I'm grateful in my subconscious, multiple times over.

I like to wake up at 7 a.m. (except after a long trip or on an off day when I have to catch up on my beauty sleep).

Waking early gives me control over my day. I absolutely refrain from checking my phone in the morning – I find it is the easiest way to hand over control of my day to someone else (and that I will not do).

I do nothing for the first 20 minutes except journal, reflect and plan my day. This is one thing that has helped me maintain equilibrium and ground myself no matter where I am or what I'm doing: journalling and the practice of gratitude. I switch on a side light or draw open a curtain slightly, bring out my yellow book and red pen, and jot down what I am grateful for and what I hope to achieve today. I also use this time to remind myself of my goals, big or small.

My family and friends call me 'aggressively positive' but I do take pride in the fact that I can find a ray of light in any situation. I genuinely believe that everything happens for a reason and it's all rigged in our favour.

In terms of my lifestyle, I have always been – and I still am – a super-active person. I grew up playing football religiously. I love to dance, play padel and go for walks. And I am not bullshitting anyone here but **the number of steps I do just pacing during my work calls is amazing** (well, the amount I talk to my clients and team on the phone explains it) because I can't sit still during calls. I don't like to work out – I haven't yet found any 'go-to movement' that I can follow religiously. My motto is to just keep moving. That's how I stay active. And it's working well for my body.

Some things people assume about me are so untrue, possibly perceived from my online persona. People think I am addicted to my phone. But I am great at distancing myself from it. If I am in a room with ten people at a party or even a recreational area somewhere, the other nine will use their phone a lot more than I will. I overuse my phone so much at work that I am at a point of exhaustion during my personal time. I crave analogue human connection. And I make sure I get it.

My idea of a holiday or a weekend or time off is strictly never to scroll social media, go to a mall or shop online. I see too many products, people and posts while I work. A beach or mountain does it for me. In fact, for most people with hectic jobs, I feel a holiday in nature is probably your best bet, way better than a holiday based on shopping. Lying on a couch with a book, catching up on Netflix shows or having dinner with a small group of friends is my idea of a weekend. I don't feel the need to keep in touch compulsively or make digital connections every day.

A GYPSY LIFE

I crave routine but I am just unable to get much of it. And that's because I wing a large part of this manic life of mine. And my job requires me to be agile and adaptable. I've learnt to embrace that over time.

I have also moved three countries in the past decade. And let me just take this moment to say that moving countries is challenging. It's an absolute uprooting of everything you know and believe – your life, your physical surroundings, the neighbourhood, the faces you see and the weather you thrive in. And each move came with its fair share of contrasts. But the one thing it inculcated in me is stone-cold adaptability. Thanks to these moves, you can put me anywhere, and I will blossom even in discomfort.

When I first moved to Belgium, I had to keep travelling to ensure that I got work. Travel sounds very glamorous, especially my type of travel. I wanted to travel three times a week and go to Paris, Milan, London. But, trust me, when I got down to it, I was physically and mentally drained. There is no routine, your food habits are all over the place, your body is in unacquainted territory every night, you don't sleep enough, you're adapting every minute, you miss the familiarity and support of your loved ones. For me, it felt glorious at the beginning but the scale and urgency with which I was doing it was unhealthy.

When I was pregnant with my son Zavi – he was born in December 2022 – I decided to uproot myself from my home in Belgium and be with my family in Mumbai for a six-month stretch. When he was three months old, I returned to Belgium and then moved to Dubai permanently, that too after shuttling between both places for a bit. The decision of moving to Dubai was a tricky one, and we spent months mulling over it. My husband and I both wanted to be in a place that would have more opportunity for our ambitions. Shailin used to travel to Dubai for work and I accompanied him on a few trips to survey the market and evaluate the potential. I spoke to a few veterans and found that there was no mega influencer (mega stands for the size of your following) with a South Asian audience and South Asians make up more than 40 per cent of the UAE population. There was a huge opportunity here and a sizeable market waiting to be captured. I was also tired of spending 70 per cent of my life zipping around for work. I wanted stability and a routine. Working while being based in Belgium meant having to constantly travel to find work because Belgium itself was not a market for me and I didn't find that ideal while building a family. Shailin's travels too would get easier and faster and my proximity to India would be a game-changer. It was a risk for us as a family but I urged Shailin to take the plunge.

WORKING GIRL GUILT

This is as good a time as any to talk about guilt. It's a truth most women live with.

I cannot honestly say I dedicate x amount of time to my husband and son every morning or night. Or that I have diarized time which is only theirs. I don't! But the one thing that I do have going for me is that I work from home. And now that I am a mom, it's one of my life's biggest luxuries.

I am so grateful for the autonomy my job gives me. The ability to have a ten-hour working day but to be able to choose what those ten hours are. The freedom to be my own boss. I can be 'at work', finish a call, open my room door and give Zavi a squeeze and kiss. I am there if he needs me. It gels really well with the excessive travelling I do because being at home helps me make up for it (the guilt). As I type this, he has come through my bedroom door and greeted me with the biggest smile on his face.

But I'll be honest. There are days when I can't keep up with any of it. When everything and anything is just too much. At the same time, it is hard for my family to work around my hectic schedule; this applies to my son, my husband, my parents and in-laws. I am so lucky that I have the privilege of help – from family and staff. And I have to be honest, I have used all the help in the world on the personal front to be able to manage my life on the professional front.

My parents and in-laws constantly feel like they have a daughter who just doesn't have enough time for them and I hate that feeling. It bogs me down with guilt.

Every time I am in Mumbai (where my parents live and my team lives and where most of my events are) my schedule is crazy. I can't give my parents enough time. It breaks my heart. I have apologized to my mom multiple times. 'I am sorry you have a daughter who is this busy,' I say, 'whose work is so time-consuming. But it's a choice I make for myself every single day.'

This is the choice that I have made. **I want to be a working woman. It means the world to me to be able to work, be productive and earn a good livelihood.**

I lost my grandmother (my nani) to Covid in late 2023. For my mom, she lost her mother. She had an extremely hard time dealing with the loss and her biggest regret through it all was not spending enough time with her mother. Despite all my determination, I can't help but be dragged into that dark hole of thoughts – what if I spend all my time working and later regretting it?

My in-laws belong to a community where it was an obstacle for them to accept a working woman in the family. But they have embraced a daughter-in-law who not only works but one who works unabashedly in a public forum as a public figure. I have deep respect for them for this, even though it has taken them some time to understand and accept it.

From the time I got engaged, I have had to explain who I am and what I do so many times over to people. There have been many, many instances where I have been absent at family events – because I am working. **It's just so much trickier for others to accept and understand my work life when I am not going into a 'corporate' office. 'She's just sitting in her room and working' – so what is she really doing, right? It doesn't add up for people.** And I get that they don't understand what I do, how it holds value, and that it isn't a 'timepass' hobby that so many Indian aunties and uncles brush it off as. **I guess many young entrepreneurs and young working professionals might find themselves in the same boat.**

I am married into a fairly devout Jain family and I can never forget the time, early into my marriage, when my husband undertook a strict eight-day no-food Jain fast called Athai, which ends with a big ritual and celebration. I lived in Belgium at the time. I had an opportunity to shoot with a fashion brand in London. I had committed to it way before Shailin undertook this fast. He understood that I needed to go. But my not being there didn't go down well with everybody else in the family. It was a huge deal. I felt so guilty on that train ride from Antwerp to London, I wept through most of the journey. But against all odds, I showed up for my work.

I hurt my in-laws and family and, somewhere along the way, I hurt myself. But you have to make these choices over and over again for yourself.

In hindsight, did that London shoot I ditched my husband's Athai celebration for bring me some insanely successful outcome? Hell, no. It was strictly average. But it was in London, at a time when getting that chance for me was a big deal; heck, doing anything internationally was such a big deal. At that moment, it felt really important. **And most significantly, it was a commitment I had made to my work. I had to show up.** If I couldn't respect a commitment I had made, how could I expect anyone in my family to respect my work?

WORK–LIFE, PERSONAL–PROFESSIONAL, LA-DI-DA

Separating my personal and professional life in my profession has been brutal. In fact, it has been almost impossible at times. There have been so many instances where I've completely lost all sense of direction because I found it so hard to distinguish between the two. I post about a visit from my family and a dinner out with friends, and my community loves it. I post my outfit from a cousin's wedding or share how I decorated my home for Diwali, and it goes viral. Having a camera on your marriage is draining. What part of my life is lived to live and what part of it is lived for my job?

I'm learning how to consciously separate the two. How to keep work during work hours. How to say no to attending an event on the weekend. How to tell my team that even though family content might perform very well, I don't feel comfortable creating it so frequently. I'm learning that even though so much of my life is shared online, it doesn't mean that *all* of it needs to be. It's a work in progress.

So when someone asks me about work–life balance – yes, I get it. And as much as I get it, I struggle to achieve it. There's no black-and-white answer to this, so I've found myself a solution that works (for now). Rather than trying to achieve 'balance' on a daily basis, I focus on doing so in the medium to long run, and I constantly remind myself of my priorities.

What are my priorities?

If I had to close my eyes and answer this question with my hand on my heart:

- Family and friends
- Work
- Health
- Personal aspirations
- Money

My priority is my family (P.S. Who comes under 'family' is my discretion). Everything after that on the above list falls short. I truly believe that there's no joy in tasting success if you're alone. And I will expand on this a little later in the chapter.

Balance, in my dictionary, is fluid. It's okay to be overworked some days or some weeks and it's also okay to have four-day work weeks and it's also okay to take a mid-year vacation. It's okay to have a hectic quarter followed by a slow one. When work beckons, YOU HAVE TO BE THERE. And when your personal life needs you,

you ALSO HAVE TO BE THERE. But in the other beautifully mundane moments, it's okay to do a little jiggle-wiggle, do a little of everything you love AND JUST LIVE.

But now that I have a baby, it is trickier. I don't expect my son to understand that Mama has had a ten-hour shoot and is exhausted. After a gruelling day's work, I still have to and want to show up for him. Even when I don't physically have the energy. But you conjure it up for your baby.

MARRIAGE, MOTHERHOOD AND OTHER RELATIONSHIPS IN BETWEEN

Everyone sees the end results. The campaigns. The hoardings. The awards. The fans. But very, very few realize what you need to put in to get that. Very often even now my family and close friends don't understand it. But it's not theirs to understand, it's mine to explain. It's for me to understand and accept that I cannot show up for everything or everyone on a daily basis. I have to say a lot of nos. I draw a tight circle. It is a choice I have consciously made.

And instead of constantly feeling torn, I am just became stingy with my energy and who gets access to it.

I thrive on low-maintenance friendships and relationships. And this isn't always agreeable to some people, who then drop away. That's fine.

I have one best friend whom I speak to religiously every single day, since the day we met; she's my sounding board and I'm beyond grateful to have that sense of sanity in a rather insane environment.

I have a few extremely close friends who I know would do anything for me. I can go three weeks without speaking to them but it's okay. **I thank my stars for these friends who understand that you're busy and that you can't keep up every day and say 'thank you for being in my life'.** They know you won't make it for everything but when you do, it is with the best intentions. I am grateful to be able to recognize these people. If you are lucky enough to have such folks in your life, hold on to them with everything you've got.

My husband and I both travel maniacally for our respective jobs. I've been crystal clear about my goals and aspirations with my husband from day one and I could not stress more how important that communication is – i.e. outlining your priorities from Day 1. We're both very ambitious and that doesn't always leave us with enough time for each other. It's discomforting. Managing our relationship and our time together becomes tricky. Every time we reunite, I always grumble, 'I miss you' and 'I don't get enough time with you' and 'I wish one of our jobs was stationary'. It is he who pacifies me saying we both have jobs we love so much. And we are lucky to have each other. We work hard and travel and come back home to each other – there is no better way than this.

There is a quote by Lord Krishna in the Bhagavad Gita that describes our approach to our relationship quite well. It says: 'Love is not possessive; it is freeing. Allow your love to create wings that enable your loved ones to soar and reach their fullest potential.'

We are independent. Sometimes too independent. There are times when I've found what other couples do or act like to be unrelatable and I've also felt the pang of 'Why don't we have that'. That deathly comparison of what we see around us and on social media and that urge to always focus on what we don't have versus what we do have. Yes, I too fall into this negative spiral. But time and, more importantly, bad times, has taught me that there is no companionship, no relationship like another. The beauty is in the unique flaws, the eccentric imperfections and the unshared shortcomings that we possess as a couple.

The only thing that gets us through every phase is communication. There are times when I need Shailin to be extra understanding that it's a busy time for me. Or for him to be more sensitive because I'm having a hard time. And I've learnt that demanding it never works. I have to sit him down and be able to communicate with compassion and explain to him how this is a really important time for my work where I need to give it my 100 per cent and how it will impact my career and the revenue I generate. And he does the same for me. He also has to commit large swathes of time to attending gem and jewellery auctions, which is something I need to understand too. Putting things into perspective for people is a great piece of relationship advice I have come to learn through my own experiences.

There had come a time when my job had become my identity. It was unhealthy. But becoming a mother helped me break away from that. It showed me so many different, uncovered versions of myself. Raw, untapped. **It taught me that work alone does not define me. My work is only a 'part' of who I am – it's not me in my entirety.**

On the tough days of motherhood, I also taught myself that motherhood too is only a 'part' of who I am – it's not me in my entirety.

I've been asked repeatedly after the birth of my son Zavi, 'It must have been hard to go back to work after having a baby, no?' But in all honesty, I now want to work harder than I ever have before. In fact, the question that keeps coming to me is, 'Am I doing enough?' Because my son has made me realize that I have the capacity, the potential to do more. He's made me realize that I am so much more than what I thought I could be.

Since my son was 40 days old, he has come along with me to shoots, sets and meetings. At first it might have been because I was breastfeeding. But gradually it became so because **I wanted him to see that his mom was working, and accept and understand that he has a mother who has a job she loves very much.**

When he grows up and his demands also increase with time and age, I think perhaps he will be able to accept my absence with grace and be supportive. That's all I can hope to instil in him.

He recently started nursery. Every time I'm out for a meeting or away on a work trip and I'm unable to be home to receive him, my heart breaks with guilt. But then I have to remind myself that my mom was not always waiting at home for me. But she was there for me, always accessible. If I didn't call my dad at his office within five minutes of being home from school, there were consequences! That was their level of availability and dependability. And I see the impact of that in the person I have become. I am so much more confident to fly because I know if I fall, they'll be there to catch me.

And the feeling of not having the fear of falling – do you know how life altering that can be?

That's the foundation I hope to build for the family I nurture.

AFTERWORD

So why did I write this book?

It might have been nice to have a story like this to listen to when I was a lost and listless college girl. **We live in the day and age of unconventional careers and yet there are such few in-depth accounts of those journeys.** And I wanted to share my story on thriving (and failing) on an offbeat path, converting my passion into my work and pointing out the jarring mistakes I made along the way – so it could make someone else's journey just a little easier.

By no means is it a story of roaring success . . .

By no means do I think 'I've made it' . . .

Because you see 'making it' will imply it's the end. It's only really the beginning.

I am often asked this by those around me: What is your biggest accomplishment? Pat come the multiple choice answers . . .

Was it when I made it to the glamorous red carpet of the Cannes Film Festival or when I made it to the Forbes '30 under 30' list? Or is it when I get recognized and stopped for photographs by fans anywhere from Paris to Bali? Or is it every time my parents get stopped when they set foot in a mall? Is it the financial abundance or the fierce confidence I've adopted over the years? Or was it becoming a mother?

None really feel like my biggest accomplishment. Because achieving your biggest goal and fulfilling your largest dream will mean I've made it. And making it would mean I don't wake up with the conviction and fire I need running through my veins when I know I haven't reached my highest peak yet.

I could be on stage at a TEDTalk or in the South of France at a Spring/Summer show or fighting with my husband or on the receiving end of some terrible public takedown the previous night, but when I wake up the next morning, I still have to show up at work. I'm in it to show up.

At the start of 2024, the buzzword across the world is that influencers are out, to quote a leading publication, 'Have we reached peak influencer?' There is so much chatter globally on this profession – lots of hate and revolt. First, everyone questioned it. Then, everyone wanted to be it. And now, people seem to despise it. Once again, I am standing at the cusp of a wave of uncertainty and I know it.

My husband often asks me, 'What will you do if Instagram shuts down?'

But I am fearless. I started a successful career on the dot.com, which has hardly any impact in today's day and age. And I'm still here. I don't find myself dependent on any platform or trend. The only person I depend on is me.

I've found that success is not permanent. Nor is failure. What is permanent is the ability to show up for myself every single day and show up with passion. To do better than I did yesterday.

I remember this one specific Shah Rukh Khan interview that deeply resonated with me and remains fresh in my mind. He was asked if he feels like he's achieved enough, if he's satisfied. He responded saying, 'I am like a mountain climber. I don't care about reaching the peak and hoisting the flag, I just want to climb. I just have to keep climbing. It's not for the ambition, it's not for the greed, it's not for success, I just want to climb.'

And that, my dear readers, is exactly how I feel. I love the climb. I live for the climb. I want to keep climbing.

'The woods are lovely, dark and deep,
But I have promises to keep,
And miles to go before I sleep,
And miles to go before I sleep.'

A NOTE ON THE AUTHOR
AND CO-AUTHOR

Masoom Minawala is one of India's first and most successful influencer-creators, with 1.4 million devoted followers. An entrepreneur and investor, she has been on *Forbes Asia*'s 30 Under 30 list, *GQ*'s Most Influential Young Indians, HSBC's list of leading female entrepreneurs worldwide, as well as CNN's 20 Under 40 list.

Aditi Shah Bhimjyani graduated from the University of Southern California, Los Angeles, with a degree in Communication and Journalism. She is a freelance writer whose work has appeared in several publications. She is the co-author of *Kareena Kapoor Khan's Pregnancy Bible*. She lives in Mumbai with her family.